Designing
Strategic Cost Systems

How to Unleash the Power of Cost Information

Lianabel Oliver

WILEY

John Wiley & Sons, Inc.

Library of Congress Cataloging-in-Publication Data:

Oliver, Lianabel.
  Designing strategic cost systems : how to unleash the power of cost information / Lianabel Oliver.
    p. cm.
  "Published simultaneously in Canada."
  Includes bibliographical references and index.
  ISBN 0-471-65358-6
  1. Cost accounting. 2. Cost control. 3. Activity-based costing. I. Title.
  HF5686.C8 O455 2004
  658.15'52–dc22
                                                        2003023871

About the Web Site

As the purchaser of this book, *Designing Strategic Cost Systems: How to Unleash the Power of Cost Information*, you have access to the supporting Web site:

www.wiley.com/go/costsystems

The password to enter this site is: **designing**

The Web site contains the following files/link:

Appendix A, Examples of Terms and Definitions (Cost_Terms.doc)

This file contains the terms and definitions that are shown in Appendix A of the book. You may copy these definitions to a word processing program and use them as a boilerplate to develop cost terminology that is unique for your organization.

Appendix B, Templates: Capacity Reporting Models (Appendix_B.Templates.xls)

This file contains three Excel worksheets that reference the figures contained in Appendix B. These worksheets can be used as templates to set up capacity reporting models in your organization:

- ○ **Figure B.4, Capacity Utilization: Tropical Blends Corporation.** This worksheet shows one possible way to report capacity utilization in hours. The data in this worksheet feeds the other two worksheets contained in this file.

- ○ **Figure B.5, CAM-I Reporting Model for Tropical Blends Corporation.** This worksheet shows the CAM-I capacity reporting model as shown in Appendix B and how to link capacity hours to dollars using this model.

○ **Figure B.6, Resource Effectiveness Model for Tropical Blends Corporation.** This worksheet presents an example of the Resource Effectiveness Model as shown in Appendix B. It shows how to tie the capacity utilization reported in hours to the costs of running the organization. In addition, it calculates the cost improvement opportunity for each capacity utilization index.

Appendix C, An Example of How to Use Monte Carlo Simulations to Set Standards (AppendixC.xls)

This file contains the Monte Carlo simulation model discussed in Appendix C. You must have Crystal Ball installed to run the Monte Carlo simulation. If not, you will just see an Excel spreadsheet. Do not try to replicate the exact results of the Monte Carlo simulation in this file. A Monte Carlo simulation generates a different set of random variables each time it is run. Therefore, the results of a particular run will be consistent, but different from a prior run.

Calculation of Total Labor Hours Available (LaborHrs_Available.xls)

This file provides a template with instructions that guide you through the calculation of labor hours available per employee as shown in Figure 6.9 in Chapter 6. You may use this template to perform this calculation for your own organization.

Download Crystal Ball

Crystal Ball is a powerful spreadsheet simulation program that functions as an Excel add-in. The Crystal Ball program must be installed on your computer in order to run the Monte Carlo simulation contained in the file called "AppendixC.xls." The link will allow you to download a free trial version of Crystal Ball from the Decisioneering Web site.

As part of the registration to this Web site, you will automatically receive an update on related titles published by John Wiley & Sons, Inc. If, after receiving this update, you decide you do not want to receive future updates, simply click the unsubscribe option at the end of the e-mail.

Contents

Foreword

Do you and your fellow managers make wise economic decisions? How do you know? Do you gather accurate cost information as a valuable means for helping make intelligent strategic and tactical moves? This book provides important information, insights, and steps that will make you a better manager and decision maker.

Designing Strategic Cost Systems is not a technical accounting treatise. It is not a cookbook. Instead, the book provides guidance for the design, development, and implementation of a strategic cost system. Such a system leads toward better strategic decisions, competitive advantage, and increased profitability.

The book aims at managers of service and manufacturing organizations. It targets a wide audience, appealing to managers, supervisors, engineers, and accountants. These individuals often may be a part of a project team.

The author, Lianabel Oliver, is an experienced consultant who specializes in cost management and who has exemplary writing skills. The prose packs plenty of useful, clear information in a small space. There are numerous examples and illustrations. The book provides a delightful meshing of the best of theory and practice, woven together in an easily understood, practical style. It takes a holistic approach to the design of a cost system versus focusing on it from a strictly accounting point of view.

The book has a major premise. A useful cost system must be geared to the users and molded to the maturity level of the organization. Some companies are simply not ready for an advanced cost system. They have neither the resources nor the receptivity to adopt leading-edge cost-management ideas. The complete organization environment—the senior management's attitudes and philosophy, the managers' culture or values, the organization's processes and systems—is pivotal to choosing the cost system that best fits the company.

No lone approach to systems design can pertain to all companies. Consequently, the book carefully explores how to develop a design process that will succeed in a given company environment.

Successive chapters examine the important aspects of designing a strategic cost system. Here are some highlights of the thorough coverage included in this book:

○ Determining whether your system is obsolete

○ Attributes of a good cost system

○ Stages of a redesign project

○ Steps in designing a cost model

○ Resolving major costing issues

○ Setting up and testing cost systems

○ Performance measurement and reporting

○ Common pitfalls

There are always costs and benefits related to the redesign of cost systems. Obviously, complexities of the system often raise costs. However, a cost system that is carefully tailored to a particular organization will pay for itself and beyond. This book can be a noteworthy bargain. Why? Because it can supply information and tools to make your cost system a source of strategic and competitive advantage.

CHARLES T. HORNGREN

Stanford Graduate School
of Business

Preface

How well do you know your costs? Do they reflect the resources consumed by your business processes? Do you trust the cost information generated by your financial systems to make key management decisions? The answers to these questions are critical to your company's long-term survival. Although traditional financial statements measure aggregate organizational performance, they are totally inadequate to identify opportunities to increase your competitiveness in the marketplace. A good cost system can provide the business intelligence to make better decisions at all levels in the organization. Whether you work in a manufacturing or service organization, cost information is key to identifying possibilities for value creation and improved profitability.

This book describes how to design your cost system to become a more effective decision-making tool and a source of strategic advantage. It is based largely on my experience as a consultant specializing in cost management. In contrast to other books or articles that you may have read on this subject, this book does not advocate a specific approach such as activity-based costing, direct costing, theory of constraints, standard costs, or Six Sigma. It is based on the premise that a good cost system should be tailored toward the needs of its users and adapted to the maturity level of the organization. A company may not have the infrastructure or the organizational readiness to support an advanced cost system. Not all companies have the resources or the desire to implement the latest and greatest in cost management thinking. The overall company environment—the interaction of people, systems, processes, and management philosophy—is a key driver in determining the type of cost system that can be implemented in any organization.

This book will provide you with a roadmap for the design, development, and implementation of a strategic cost system. However, there is no single approach that can be applied to all organizations. Each company should develop a process that will work in its particular environment. This book will describe how to structure a cost systems design project and discusses the issues that should be addressed upfront from a management, operations, and costing perspective. It is addressed toward senior managers who may be evaluating a cost system redesign project for their organization and business professionals such as managers, supervisors, engineers, and accountants who may form part of the project team.

How do you know if you need a new cost system? Chapter 1 addresses this issue. It presents the different functions of a cost system in an organization and the trade-offs that may be involved when one system is used to satisfy different business objectives. It discusses the internal and external manifestations of a dysfunctional cost system and how it may be affecting your organization's performance and competitive position. Finally, it identifies those situations that should trigger a revision of your cost system to ensure that it properly reflects changes in the operating environment.

Chapter 2 defines a strategic cost system and describes its major elements and attributes. Many cost systems are a byproduct of the financial accounting system. They were established under a traditional framework for the purpose of valuing inventory and recording cost of sales. From a financial accounting perspective, the individual product or service cost accuracy is of secondary importance as long as the aggregate numbers reported on financial statements are properly stated. In addition, cost systems, particularly in manufacturing organizations, are often a legacy of a bricks-and-mortar economy where operational control was managed through the use of standard costs and variance analysis. The rapid technological changes of the past 30 years, and in particular of the last decade, have made this accounting model obsolete. Yet many companies continue to use standard costs and variance analysis to manage their business. For example, in the pharmaceutical industry, the financial performance of the manufacturing sites are often evaluated using a metric called the *absorption variance.*[1] The excessive focus on this performance measure often leads to dysfunctional management behavior and suboptimizes the use of company resources. Chapter 2 also explains the six major elements that make up a cost system and how these elements interact to produce reliable and accurate cost information. In addition, it discusses those key attributes that determine the usefulness of a cost system as a decision-making tool.

Chapter 3 revolves around the redesign process. The material presented in this chapter will probably seem very familiar. A cost system redesign is a major project, and like any project, it should address certain needs, have well-defined objectives, and produce specific deliverables. This chapter will describe the different project stages and how to organize the project to increase its probabilities of success. The process discussed in this chapter is not unique to a cost system redesign project, but will be discussed from this perspective.

Chapter 4 explains the steps involved in developing the system design and details the major milestones and tasks that should be accomplished at this stage. The completion of these milestones prior to the system setup will ensure consistency in the data collection process and minimize wasted time and effort in reworking information.

Chapter 5 shows how to calculate the costs of a product or service. If you are familiar with costing processes, you may wish to skim over this chapter. However, understanding the major cost components and how they are put together is a fundamental building block of any cost system. In addition, understanding the current costing methodology and its inadequacies is a starting point for any cost system redesign project.

Chapter 6 presents the significant issues that should be addressed during the development of the costing methodology and subsequent system setup and test. These issues relate to capacity utilization, yield or process efficiency, data analysis, labor productivity, cost types, and costing methods. The discussion and resolution of issues will determine the accuracy and usefulness of your cost information. It will also provide managers with a better understanding of the organization's cost structure and how policies, procedures, and past decisions affect the reported costs.

Once you have designed a system, you must test and implement it. Chapter 7 deals with implementation issues. This is the hardest part of a cost system redesign project. Often, projects die before they even reach this stage. The implementation process requires time, effort, and persistence. It demands the support of key users in operations, accounting, and of course, information systems. Information systems will be a key player at this stage of the process. In this chapter, we will present some guidelines on how to manage the implementation process to increase its chances of success and minimize the organizational pain that may be involved with the establishment of a new system.

Chapter 8 discusses performance measurement as an integral part of a cost management system. Performance measures link strategy to execution;

a cost system ties this execution to its financial implications. A target of a 95 percent customer satisfaction level will place very different demands on the organization's resources than a target of 80 percent. The cost system integrates strategy, measurement, and financial performance in a holistic manner so that management can tie strategy and execution with the financial results of the organization.

Chapter 9 discusses the common pitfalls of a cost system redesign project. It presents major obstacles or challenges that can undermine a cost redesign project and eventually lead to its demise. It also suggests proactive measures that a team can take to ensure that the cost system is successfully implemented and withstands the test of time.

Chapter 10 summarizes the key themes that are threaded throughout this book. First, you must be committed. A cost system redesign is a major undertaking. The major players in the organization must be staunch supporters of the project, particularly its top management and the members of the project team. I have worked with organizations in which top management verbally expresses its commitment to the project, but refuses to allocate any incremental people or funds for its execution. Actions speak louder than words. Second, you must have a realistic timeframe. Your cost system did not become obsolete overnight and will not be fixed overnight. The implementation timeframe depends on a number of factors: the number and expertise of the personnel assigned to the project, the availability and accessibility of operational data, the state of your information systems, and the stability of your organizational environment. Third, you must understand the limitations and constraints that will place boundaries on the project. These restrictions may be physical constraints such as the capabilities of your information systems or policy and procedural constraints as determined by management or corporate mandates. Fourth, you should mix and match different interdisciplinary approaches to develop a cost model that makes sense for your business. Do not fall in love with any one approach that may not be appropriate for your particular organization. Finally, you must provide for a mechanism to review your cost system on a periodic basis to ensure that it reflects current business conditions and does not become obsolete over time.

Three appendices supplement the material covered in this book. Appendix A provides an example of cost terms and definitions that can be used as a starting point to develop cost terminology for your organization. Appendix B discusses time-based capacity models and how they can be linked with cost information to highlight opportunities for improvement. Appendix C describes the use of Monte Carlo simulations to incorporate the effects of uncertainty in setting time standards.

This book will address the needs of both service and manufacturing organizations. As mentioned previously, cost systems were developed primarily to address the needs of a bricks-and-mortar economy rooted in manufacturing. As we move toward a knowledge-based economy, we must learn to apply these concepts within a different context. Although the linkage is not as straightforward, most concepts that have traditionally been used in manufacturing are equally appropriate for the service and knowledge-based sector.

A good cost system is an investment that pays for itself. It allows you to identify opportunities to create value for the customer and increase shareholder wealth. This book will provide you with the tools to transform your cost system into a source of competitive advantage for your organization.

ENDNOTE

1. This variance measures the difference between actual and standard labor and overhead costs incurred in a particular time period. The standard cost of the products is "absorbed" into inventory; the difference between the actual and standard costs—the absorption variance—is usually charged to cost of sales.

Acknowledgments

This book integrates the ideas and experience of many individuals over the course of a decade. I would like to acknowledge the many people who have helped develop the ideas set forth in this book and have allowed their companies to become a living lab to experiment with innovative approaches to costing problems.

First, I would like to thank Dr. Charles Horngren, emeritus professor at Stanford University, for his constant support and invaluable insight based on years of accumulated experience in this field. I am also deeply grateful to my husband, Dr. Ricardo Gonzalez, professor in the Department of Radiological Sciences at the University of Puerto Rico Medical Sciences Campus, who significantly contributed to refining the statistical concepts presented in this book.

I would also like to recognize the contribution of other individuals who have worked with me over the years and have exposed me to ideas on how to address difficult costing or operational issues:

○ The cost model project team at ICN Pharmaceuticals in Humacao, Puerto Rico: José Vázquez, Myrna Aponte, Sammy Pérez, Denise Rodríguez, and Gizela Cintrón. Their persistence and constancy of purpose allowed the successful completion of a project that worked against tremendous odds. I would also like to thank the controller, Vance White, and the general manager, Francisco Gutiérrez, for their unwavering support of this project.

○ Santos Sanabria and Janet Rodríguez of Pfizer Inc. in Caguas, Puerto Rico. Santos introduced me to the use of Monte Carlo simulations for standards setting, and his ideas are incorporated in Appendix C of this book. Janet was an invaluable teacher in explaining production operations and working through the costing implications for their facility.

○ Peter Lectora, Rafael Vassallo, and Salvador "Chiry" Vassallo of Vassallo Industries who entrusted me with the redesign of their company's cost system. Their openness to new and different ways of looking at the business allowed us to develop a unique solution tailored to their particular operating environment.

o Alba Figueroa, now with Ocular Science Inc., who was instrumental in the development of the cost model successfully implemented at Vassallo Industries.

o My dear friend and colleague Manuel Cidre of Los Cidrines, who has been my ad hoc marketing department over the years and a great teacher of the issues and difficulties faced by an entrepreneur in developing and growing his company.

o José Luis Rosado (retired) and Raúl Cermeño of GlaxoSmithKline in Cidra, Puerto Rico. GlaxoSmithKline was my first client when I initially started my consulting practice. I am grateful for the trust they placed in my abilities and for the opportunity to receive an intensive education on the pharmaceutical industry. I would also like to thank Griselle Díaz and Daniel Nieves who were my teachers and co-facilitators in this project.

o Reinaldo Cruz, Jorge Marcano, Félix Mateo, Félix Mendoza, Mario Morales, Luis Planas, and Sophia Seda of Bacardi Corporation Puerto Rico. These individuals devoted a significant amount of time and energy to the development of the cost model implemented at Bacardi Corporation Puerto Rico. This model is unique because it is based on actual costs.

o Richard Carrión of Popular Inc. for opening the doors to the inner workings of a large financial institution. I would also like to thank the Finance team of Popular Inc.—Amílcar Jordán, Ileana González, Iris Reyes, Susie Vendrell, Luis Pérez, and Luis Abreu—and the Human Resources team—Tere Loubriel, Ivelisse Fernández, and Camelia Cestero—for their continued help and support over the diverse projects we have undertaken together at their institution.

o My Stanford classmates, Leroy Barnes and Debi Coleman, for their help and support of my first book and their helpful suggestions in this endeavor.

I would like to give special thanks to Sheck Cho, executive editor; Jennifer Hanley, senior production editor; and the staff at John Wiley & Sons, Inc. for providing me with their expert guidance and direction to ensure the completion of this project in a smooth and efficient manner. I am also indebted to Ray O'Connell, former senior acquisition editor at AMACOM Books, who was a steadfast supporter of my first book and patiently endured the growing pains of a first-time author.

Finally, I would like to thank all my clients and seminar participants, who provide me with constant challenges and opportunities that allow me to learn and grow as a person and as a business professional.

This book is dedicated to Professor Charles Horngren in recognition of his outstanding contributions to the field of management accounting.

1

Is Your Cost System Obsolete?

Most organizations have some type of system in place to calculate and report costs. These systems vary in degrees of complexity and sophistication, from the simple spreadsheet model running on a standalone computer to an integrated enterprise application running on a server or mainframe system. These cost systems are usually based on a set of assumptions about the operating environment that drives the cost calculations. These assumptions, as well as the cost calculation methodology, determine the accuracy of the cost information and its reliability and relevance for management decision making.

Once organizations develop a cost model and standardize the methodology, these practices are rarely reexamined or revisited. However, if the operational data that underlie the cost calculations are not updated on a continual basis and the costing methodology is not aligned to the business processes, a cost system will rapidly fall into obsolescence. This situation occurred in the late 1970s and early 1980s, when manufacturers based their cost calculations on direct labor hours despite the increased automation of their business processes. The lack of a clear relationship between the business processes and the output generated by the cost system created serious distortions in the information reported and resulted in a loss of credibility for management accountants. In many organizations, cost systems became dysfunctional tools that had little value for management decision making. Kaplan and Johnson brought this issue to the forefront with their book *Relevance Lost.*[1]

Obsolete cost systems are the result of evolutionary changes in the business processes and procedures that are not incorporated in the costing practices of the organization. These cost systems become outdated and no longer support the strategic direction of the organization. Dysfunctional cost systems have impaired or abnormal functioning. They do not work as designed and often encourage suboptimal behaviors among managers and employees. Obsolete cost systems are usually dysfunctional, but not all dysfunctional cost systems are obsolete.

Obsolete, dysfunctional cost systems do not develop overnight and manifest symptoms that are often difficult to ignore. The deterioration process is gradual and often goes unnoticed. Usually external pressures will force management to take a hard look at the company's cost system in order to remain competitive.

Dysfunctional cost systems manifest symptoms that are often difficult to ignore. In this chapter, we will discuss the common manifestations of obsolete, dysfunctional cost systems. Some of these warning signs are documented in the accounting literature and others are based on situations that I have come across in my consulting practice. Before we discuss these symptoms, however, we must understand the functions of a cost system in an organization and the trade-offs that may be involved when one system is used to satisfy different business objectives. Such multiplicity of purposes often results in inadequate cost systems that ultimately fall into obsolescence.

FUNCTIONS OF A COST SYSTEM

Organizations generally establish a cost system to serve several purposes. Kaplan addressed this issue by identifying three major functions of a cost system:[2]

1. *Inventory valuation* involves the periodic allocation of production cost between cost of goods sold and inventory.

2. *Operational control* provides feedback to managers on the resources consumed.

3. *Individual product cost measurement* addresses the development of unit costs for goods manufactured.

Kaplan argued that no one single system could adequately address the demands made by the diverse functions of a cost system and therefore proposed the use of multiple cost systems to satisfy the different needs for cost information.

Kaplan was strongly criticized by accounting practitioners who argued that multiple cost systems were not practical or economically feasible in the real world. Subsequently, he published an article in which he describes the four stages of a cost system, with the final stage being an integrated cost management system that could address the multiple demands for cost information made by its users.[3] The harsh reality is that for most companies, one cost system must be enough.

As initially described by Kaplan, the functions of a cost system revolved around manufacturing where the activity-based costing revolution began. However, the functions of a cost system are broader than those described by Kaplan. Figure 1.1 shows the functions of a cost system in service and manufacturing organizations and the type of information that is provided by each function. Cost systems serve four major purposes in an organization:

Figure 1.1 Major Function of a Cost System

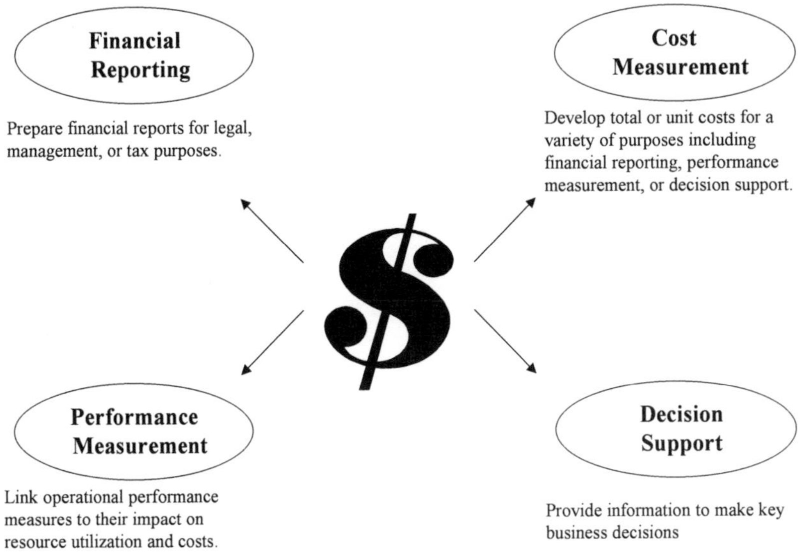

Financial Reporting

Prepare financial reports for legal, management, or tax purposes.

Cost Measurement

Develop total or unit costs for a variety of purposes including financial reporting, performance measurement, or decision support.

Performance Measurement

Link operational performance measures to their impact on resource utilization and costs.

Decision Support

Provide information to make key business decisions

1. *Financial reporting.* This function involves financial reporting for management, legal, and tax purposes. It has been the primary focus of many cost systems for decades. In manufacturing organizations, the emphasis is on inventory valuation and the allocation of manufacturing costs between inventory and cost of goods sold. In service organizations, it may involve transfer pricing or cost allocations so that subunits of the organization pay their fair share of the costs incurred to deliver a service.

2. *Cost measurement.* This function entails developing costs, per unit or in total, for a variety of different items—products, services, customers, projects, programs, departments, or work areas. Manufacturing organizations tend to be more advanced in costing procedures than service organizations due to the focus of cost accounting practices on manufacturing entities. With the rise of a service economy based on knowledge and information, the need to cost services has risen dramatically. It is no longer acceptable to manage service organizations in the aggregate. Cost information is important to determine the mix of services and customer profitability similar to manufacturing organizations.

3. *Performance management.* In the past, accountants attempted to control the business processes through the use of standard costs and variance analysis.[4] Increased automation has placed operational control where it should be—in the hands of the manager who is accountable for results. A cost system should not be focused on analyzing the past, but in making the critical link among operational measures, resource utilization, and costs in order to impact the future. It should be a tool to help manage organizational performance. In this function, most cost systems are severely lacking.

4. *Decision support.* Cost systems should provide information to make key decisions such as subcontracting services, product expansion or divestiture, capital investments, and many others. Many companies use full costs for these types of decisions.[5] However, this type of cost may be not appropriate for a particular situation and may in fact lead to the selection of a suboptimal alternative. The following situation illustrates this point. One of my clients used full

costs to subcontract the manufacturing of an unprofitable product. These costs included fixed overhead, which the company would incur regardless of whether they produced this product. When the owner informed me of his decision and showed me the cost analysis, I pointed out that he would probably expect to see a further deterioration of his financial results as a consequence of this action. The following month bore out my prediction—the company experienced a dramatic reduction in net income. At the time the decision was made, the sales price of the product covered its variable costs and contributed to the recovery of the fixed overhead costs of the facility. With the outsourcing decision, the company decreased the net incremental sales revenue of the subcontracted product but continued to incur the fixed costs of its manufacturing facility.[6] This situation resulted in a deterioration of the cash flow position and financial performance of the organization.

The key to designing a strategic cost system is understanding what are the most important functions for your organization and how much you are willing to invest to make it work. A cost system may be perfectly adequate for financial reporting purposes, but totally inadequate for cost measurement or decision support. Data collection and maintenance also have a cost, so the more cost information you require, the more resources you will need to develop and maintain the system. You may choose to design a system that is less precise and less integrated with operational measures, but captures the essence of your organization's cost structure with a lower investment of time and resources. The design of cost systems involves a trade-off between precision and the costs of data collection and maintenance. You must ensure that the system satisfies the critical business needs without placing an undue burden on the organization.

SYMPTOMS OF A DYSFUNCTIONAL COST SYSTEM

Although your cost system may not be obsolete, it might be creating dysfunctional behavior in your organization. The deterioration of a cost system is a gradual progression: processes change, people leave, and knowledge is lost. The day-to-day activities consume the time, energy, and focus of the

Figure 1.2 Symptoms of a Dysfunctional Cost System

Internal Warning Signs	External Warning Signs
1. Users complain that the financial reports are inaccurate or do not reflect the reality of the business operations.	1. Customers accept price increases without complaint.
2. Managers cannot explain the financial results.	2. Competitor prices are equal to your costs.
3. Managers do not use financial reports.	3. Supplier bids are lower than expected.
4. Managers develop their own cost models.	4. You have no competitors in a particular market niche.
5. Managers want to drop seemingly profitable products or services.	
6. Accountants spend a lot of time on special analyses or requests.	
7. Inconsistency in reported data.	
8. Managers engage in suboptimal decision making.	

organization. Nonessential activities such as updating operational standards, reviewing processes and procedures, or revising the cost methodology are put on the back burner.

The warning signs of a dysfunctional cost system are unmistakable.[7] I have categorized the warning signs into two major groups: internal and external manifestations. Internal manifestations are those that occur within the organization and are usually communicated by an internal user such as a department manager or project engineer. External manifestations are signals provided by our customers or suppliers that something is seriously amiss with the cost system. Figure 1.2 summarizes the internal and external warning signs of an obsolete cost system.

Internal Warning Signs

1. *Users complain that the financial reports are inaccurate or do not reflect the reality of the business operations.* When financial results are out of line with management expectations, it may be a signal that the cost system is not capturing the reality of the business processes. Accountants need to investigate whether the problem lies in operations, accounting, or both areas. For example, is it an error in the

product or process specifications? Is it a problem with the cost assignment methodology? Is it a combination of operational and accounting issues? The result of this investigation may uncover the next warning sign.

2. *Managers cannot explain the financial results.* Managers should be able to give simple explanations for their profit margins and costs. If your management cannot explain the financial results, it is time to take a hard look at how you are reporting the numbers. Sometimes even the accountants cannot explain the financial results. Although accountants can usually trace the debits and credits and provide you with an accounting explanation of the numbers reported, they sometimes cannot articulate a clear explanation *from a business perspective.* This situation often signals a disassociation between the cost system and the underlying business processes it purports to represent, leading to the next warning sign.

3. *Managers do not use financial reports.* I have walked into several companies where the operational managers stack the financial reports in a corner. When queried on the usefulness of these reports, they voice several complaints that (a) the reports are too late, (b) the information is stale, (c) the reported costs do not reflect the true costs of the operation, and (d) they are too difficult to understand. Some companies are more diligent than others about forcing their managers to use financial reports. However, in companies where this discipline does not exist, financial reports just gather dust.

4. *Managers develop their own cost models.* If nonfinancial managers do not agree with the methodology to estimate costs, they will develop and use their own cost models. I have seen this phenomenon repeated time and time again over the course of many years. Sometimes, this situation develops into a "he said, she said" between accountants and the users that they allegedly support.

5. *Managers want to drop seemingly profitable products or services.* Managers know the time and resources that are required to deliver a service or manufacture a product, regardless of what the cost system is telling them. A low-volume product, for example, may be more costly than a high-volume product, even though it requires the

same amount of labor, materials, and process time. Because the product is produced only sporadically, it involves a learning curve each time the product is manufactured. The cost system may fail to capture the true costs of the product if this learning curve is not factored into the cost equation.

6. *Accountants spend a lot of time on special analyses or requests.* A cost system should provide managers with the information they need on a regular basis. Routine requests for cost information should not be a major undertaking. When simple requests consistently turn into special projects, it may signal that your cost system is inadequate to satisfy the basic information needs of the organization.

7. *Inconsistency in reported data.* Many financial transactions are recorded using operational data such as units sold, units produced, process hours, labor hours, or transactions processed. When the operational data shown in management reports does not tie to the operational data used to record transactions in the general ledger, there may be a serious problem lurking in your cost accounting system. It may signal a breakdown in your data collection procedures or a change in the business that is not being properly accounted for by your costing methodology or accounting procedures.

8. *Managers engage in suboptimal decision making.* This situation occurs when the design of the cost system encourages managers to make decisions that are contrary to the best interests of the organization. For example, operations managers may inflate time and yield standards to meet targeted performance levels for the business unit, not understanding the impact of this decision on the pricing or marketing strategies of the organization. Cost allocation and transfer pricing systems, which organizations use to assign costs to different business units for performance measurement and tax purposes, may also create inefficiencies in the work environment and lead to suboptimal decisions. I have seen companies where service units engage in endless negotiations with their internal clients, often delaying projects and resulting in a waste of precious management resources. In its worst manifestations, the business unit manager opts to use a third-party service provider because the internal supplier is "too expensive."

External Warning Signs

1. *Customers accept price increases without complaint.* Customers know the value of your products and services. When they accept a price increase without much objection, it may be a signal that you are underpricing your products. One of my clients was simply floored when a customer accepted a price increase that was almost double what had been previously charged for the service. When this type of situation happens, it may signal that your customer understands your costs better than you do.

2. *Competitor prices are equal to your costs.* One of my clients repeatedly encountered this symptom. Its competitors not only outbid them for orders, but their prices were equal to my client's production cost.

3. *Supplier bids are lower than expected.* When outsourcing a product or service, a company can compare the bid to the cost of providing the product or service internally. If the supplier's bid is significantly lower than your costs and they use similar technologies and processes, your cost system might be providing inaccurate information.

4. *You have no competitors in a particular market niche.* Unless you operate in a monopolistic environment or have high barriers to entry, you should expect competition. If you have a highly profitable niche all to yourself, your cost system might be reporting artificially high margins.

If your cost system is manifesting one or more of these warning signals, you should evaluate whether a system redesign is called for. Obviously, these symptoms manifest themselves in degrees of severity. Some symptoms may be more severe and signal a higher business risk than others.

NEED FOR REDESIGN

Even if your cost system is not manifesting any of the symptoms previously discussed, you may still want to review your system design and setup. Cooper has identified several situations that call for a review of your cost system to which I have added a few of my own.[8] (See Figure 1.3.)

Figure 1.3 Events That Usually Trigger a Cost System Review

- Introduction of new technology
- Changes in the use of support functions
- Changes in marketing strategy
- Changes to the business processes
- Increased competition
- Deregulation
- Changes in desired behavioral goals
- Organizational change

1. *Introduction of new technology.* Whether the technology is disruptive, such as the Internet, or an evolution from your current technology platform, the introduction of new technology requires that you revisit your business processes and understand how these are being captured by your cost system.

2. *Changes in the use of support functions.* A new product or service may cause a shift in the type or amount of resources that it demands from its support functions. A change in the business process or customer specifications may also change the support requirements of a particular product or service. Any change in the use of support functions should prompt a revision of how the costs of these resources are being assigned to the products, services, or different operating units.

3. *Changes in the marketing strategy.* If you are changing the focus of your marketing strategy, for example, to bundle or unbundle products or to emphasize a particular market niche, be sure your cost system is correctly reporting the profit margins for these products. A cost system may underestimate the cost of serving a particular market. At one of my employers, the sales and marketing division decided to market a unique product to a specific geographic region. On paper, the product looked very profitable with a high gross margin.[9] When I talked to the controller of the manufacturing facility, he was quite distressed by this new strategy. Apparently,

there were many hidden costs not reflected in the gross margin of the product. Because the product was only scheduled for production once or twice a year, there was a significant learning curve involved with each production run. In addition, the sales and marketing division would place orders of approximately 500 units a year, but the manufacturing facility could only produce it in lots of 2,500 units per year. The inventory carrying costs as well as the risks of obsolescence were not reflected in the unit cost, generating an artificially high margin for this product.

4. *Changes to the business processes.* Any significant change to the business process should be reflected in the costs. You must ensure that the change has been incorporated into the operational parameters that drive the cost calculations, and is being properly accounted for by your costing methodology as well as the accounting and data collection procedures of your operations.

5. *Increased competition.* If your competition intensifies, costs become a matter of life and death. Your company cannot afford to make mistakes, because your competitor will be there to fill in the gap.

6. *Deregulation.* Deregulation opens the door to increased competition. Accurate knowledge of costs becomes vital in identifying market opportunities and increasing overall profit levels.

7. *Changes in desired behavioral goals.* If management wants to encourage a different type of behavior in its employees, it must ensure that its cost system will promote the desired behavior. Suppose a company wanted to encourage the use of common parts in the design of new products. If the cost system does not differentiate between the costs of a common versus a unique component, an engineer will have little incentive to use common parts because there is no visible cost differential. A word of caution—be very careful when you use a cost system to promote behavioral change. Dysfunctional consequences can ensue. In the example given here, design engineers may start trading off functionality or quality by using common parts, which will make the product less attractive to the customer. The behavioral consequence of a cost system must be looked at in its entirety—not only the costing methodology, but

also the information it feeds into other management subsystems such as transfer pricing and performance measurement.

8. *Organizational change.* Whenever there is a major change in the organizational structure of a company, the cost system should be reexamined to ensure it still reflects the management philosophy, information needs, and business processes of the organization. If the change is the result of a merger and acquisition, a reevaluation of the cost system becomes imperative to ensure that all subunits of the organization are capturing and reporting costs in a consistent manner.

Cost systems are dynamic; they should change and evolve with the business. Any major change to a process, product, service, or business strategy should prompt a review of your cost system. The review process should be done at least once a year. It does not have to be a major undertaking. However, it should be sufficiently thorough to ensure that the cost system is accurately capturing the costs of your operations, encouraging the desired employee behavior, and meeting the needs of its users.

SUMMARY

The redesign of a cost system is a major undertaking that requires a significant amount of time and resources. Before embarking on a project of this magnitude, you should evaluate the information needs of the organization and where the current cost system is failing. Although your cost system may be showing symptoms of wear and tear, it could just need a tune-up versus a major engine overhaul. It is far easier to modify the system as the business evolves than to revamp the entire system in a one-time initiative. Herein lies the importance of reviewing the adequacy of your cost system on a regular basis. In the remaining chapters of this book, we will guide you through the steps of a cost system redesign, whether you just need a tweak or a major repair.

ENDNOTES

1. H. Thomas Johnson and Robert S. Kaplan, *Relevance Lost: The Rise and Fall of Management Accounting* (Boston: Harvard Business School Press, 1987).
2. Robert S. Kaplan, "One Cost System Isn't Enough," *Harvard Business Review* (January–February 1988).
3. Robert S. Kaplan, "The Four-Stage Model of Cost Systems Design," *Management Accounting* (February 1990): 22–27.
4. *Variance analysis* is the process that examines the differences between actual and standard or budgeted costs to determine their underlying causes and identify opportunities for cost improvement.
5. *Full costs* are the sum of all resources required to manufacture a product or deliver a service. In manufacturing organizations, it is the sum of labor, materials, and overhead. In service organizations, it is the sum of labor, ingredients, supplies, and other indirect costs involved in providing a service.
6. Accountants use the term *contribution margin* to describe the net incremental sales revenue. It is defined as the sales price less the variable cost per unit.
7. Robin Cooper was one of the first individuals to describe the symptoms of an obsolete cost accounting system in his article, "You Need a New Cost System When...," *Harvard Business Review* (January–February 1989). I have summarized these symptoms in this section and added a few of my own based on my experience in this area. Because cost accounting systems are usually integrated to the financial and operational control systems of the organization, these warning signals may also be indicative of a larger problem with your financial accounting and internal control system. For a more detailed discussion, see Lianabel Oliver, *The Cost Management Toolbox: A Manager's Guide to Controlling Costs and Boosting Profits* (New York: AMACOM Books, 2000), 10–12.

8. See Cooper, "You Need a New Cost System When...."
9. *Gross margin* is the difference between sales and cost of sales. It represents the amount of money left over after deducting the cost of goods sold that is available to cover operating expenses. It is usually reported on a total and per unit basis.

2

What Constitutes a Strategic Cost System?

Not all cost systems are created equal. Some cost systems are better than others in meeting the needs of their users and providing information for management decision making. In addition, as we saw in the prior chapter, some cost systems show clear signs of aging and obsolescence. Many organizations reengineer their business processes and forget to revamp the accounting systems and procedures that support these processes. This situation often results in distorted costs and large adjustments to the financial statements at the end of a reporting period.

So what are the elements of a good cost system? What key attributes will determine its usefulness and longevity? In this chapter, we will discuss the six major elements that comprise a strategic cost system. We will also explore the attributes of these systems and how you can design them into your costing processes.

WHAT IS A STRATEGIC COST SYSTEM?

A strategic cost system satisfies the legal and management requirements for financial information and supports the strategic objectives of the organization. It should accurately reflect the business processes and meet the needs of its users in a timely manner. It should provide relevant information for management decision making and elicit changes to organizational processes, procedures, and employee behavior that will eventually lead to increased margins, lower costs, higher quality, and improved customer service.

A cost system does not have to incorporate advanced cost management practices to be considered strategic. In a 2003 survey of management accounting practices conducted by the Institute of Management Accountants (IMA) and Ernst & Young (E&Y), respondents indicated that while there is a great need for accurate cost information, adopting new cost management tools is not a priority in the current economic environment.[1] The finding coincides with my own experience, where I have been asked to design cost systems that can work within the current operating environment of the organization.

ELEMENTS OF A STRATEGIC COST SYSTEM

Figure 2.1 shows the elements of a strategic cost system and the role that each element plays within it. A strategic cost system consists of six major elements:

1. *Costing methodology.* The methods used to cost products and services.
2. *Data.* The operational and financial information that supports the cost calculation.
3. *Procedures.* The accounting and operational procedures used to record actual data into the general ledger or its subsystems.
4. *Systems applications.* The software available to gather, store, and report data.
5. *Performance indicators.* The measures that will be used to evaluate managerial performance.
6. *Reports.* The operational and financial reports that are required by the business.

For a cost system to work effectively as a financial and managerial tool, all six elements must work together to provide information that is relevant, timely, and accurate. When one element is weak or inconsistent with another element, it hinders the ability of the cost system to gather, analyze, and report cost information and hence provide an effective decision-making tool. In the section below, we will explain in more detail each element and how it can affect the design and functionality of your cost system.

Figure 2.1 Elements of a Strategic Cost System

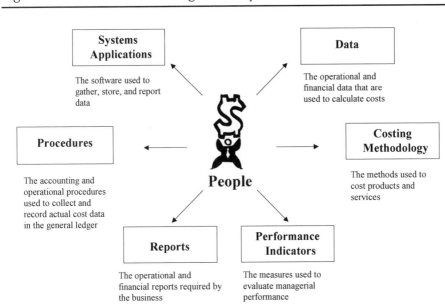

Costing Methodology

The costing methodology describes how the organization costs its products and services. It defines the major cost components and how each element is calculated and reported. In traditional manufacturing organizations, for example, product costs are usually broken down by labor, materials, and overhead.[2] High-technology manufacturers that have low labor and high overhead costs may choose to calculate and report costs into just two categories: materials and conversion costs (i.e., the sum of labor and overhead). Service organizations vary in terms of how they calculate and report costs. For example, professional service organizations may segregate the cost of their billable hours into labor and overhead, which are its major cost components. Other organizations may break down overhead into several components such as depreciation, maintenance and repair, supplies, and other. Still other organizations calculate costs without separating individual cost components on a regular basis.

Whatever methodology is used to calculate costs, it should be well-defined and clearly documented. The documentation will ensure that the methodology can be replicated in subsequent time periods in a consistent manner. It also facilitates the training of new employees as people leave the organization or are transferred to other areas.

Data

Cost calculations are based on financial and operational data that reflect how resources are consumed by a product or service. Financial data usually consist of the actual, budgeted, or estimated costs that are recorded somewhere in the accounting system on a total or per unit basis. This information can be found in the general ledger, the annual budget, or a financial forecast. Sometimes, the cost information resides in another subsystem such as payroll or inventory management, which feeds the general ledger. Calculations can also be based on estimates or benchmarks such as vendor quotes, industry averages, or best practices. For cost calculations to be accurate, they must be based on accurate financial information.

Accurate financial information, however, is only one part of the equation. In a cost calculation we quantify, in monetary terms, the resources used to deliver a product or a service. The line managers of an organization usually determine the quantity of resources required to manufacture a product or deliver a service and document these resources in a product or process specification sheet. Sometimes this determination is done in a scientific manner using quantitative methods such as statistical sampling and time studies. At other times, it is a guesstimate based on prior experience or an expert's judgment. If the operational data are inaccurate, unreliable, or outdated, accurate financial information will not produce meaningful costs. As the old saying goes, "Garbage in, garbage out." I have witnessed firsthand companies that rely on obsolete time standards or bills of materials to calculate their costs. Then their managers wonder why the cost numbers are too high, too low, or not in line with their expectations based on their knowledge of operations.

Accurate and reliable cost information requires high-quality financial and operational data. These data are the fundamental building blocks of a cost calculation and a critical element of any cost system.

Procedures

Accounting procedures capture and report the financial data that is generally used to calculate costs. When an organization develops or updates its costing methodology, it must examine the accounting procedures to ensure that they collect and report data in a manner that is consistent with the proposed changes. Although a costing methodology can be developed independently of the numbers in the general ledger, typically accountants use these numbers as a starting point when developing product or service costs. If the accounting procedures do not support the costing methodology, any unit cost information developed with this information may be inaccurate. At a minimum, the information may have to be recast in a different format before it can be used to develop costs. One of my clients had organized its departmental cost centers by customer. The redesign of its cost system involved restructuring the general ledger by production facility to facilitate the capture of actual costs using the new costing methodology.

Many companies establish unit costs during the annual budgeting process. Sometimes the accounting procedures used in the budget differ from the accounting procedures used to collect and report actual data at the beginning of the new fiscal year. This situation sets the stage for inaccurate costs. For example, suppose a department such as building maintenance was distributed to other departments in the budget based on an estimated percentage of time spent supporting an operating unit. The accounting department, however, has always distributed building maintenance based on square footage and continues this process at the start of the new fiscal year. This inconsistency in accounting procedures between budgeted and actual costs will generate costing inaccuracies that will be reflected in budget or cost variances during the fiscal year. Moreover, the comparison of actual and expected costs will not be meaningful because they were prepared using different accounting procedures that affect the costing methodology.

Operational procedures can also affect cost information. Many transactions recorded in the general ledger originate from operational areas such as material usage, labor hours consumed, units produced or sold, and line items shipped, among others. If the employees responsible for entering and maintaining this information do not follow the established data entry procedures or perform these incorrectly, these errors will eventually result in inaccurate financial information.

Moreover, operational procedures must be consistent with the established costing methodology. At one of my clients, quality samples taken from the production line were entered into the production control system as good output. Once these samples were inspected by the Quality Control (QC) department, they were scrapped in the system and physically destroyed. The accountants, however, had correctly excluded QC samples from the standard output per lot in setting the cost standards. The end result in the general ledger was a very favorable yield variance when the production order closed, partly offset by a very unfavorable scrap variance in subsequent months. Not only was cost information distorted, but also the high scrap costs generated a lot of attention from their corporate headquarters. It was during the cost redesign project that we uncovered the source of the problem—an inconsistency between the data entry procedures in manufacturing and the costing methodology used by accounting.

Cost system designers should review the accounting and operational procedures that support the established costing methodology. Any error, inconsistency, or omission will eventually translate into inaccurate cost information, particularly if it is not uncovered in a timely manner.

Systems Applications

The systems application is critical in determining the ease of computation, the access, and the availability of information of your cost system. A cost system often uses information that is stored in other applications to calculate costs. In manufacturing companies, the cost system draws on information stored in the bill of materials, the item master, and the routing file to calculate product costs.[3] Service organizations have time standards for critical processes that are stored in a planning or customer management system. Therefore, it is very important that accountants understand which subsystems affect their costing process, how these subsystems were set up, and how they might impact the cost calculations.

All costing applications, which are part of a larger enterprise system, have their limitations. Unless you decide to develop a custom solution, which is an expensive and time-consuming alternative, you will probably have to make trade-offs between the design of your cost model and how it must be set up to run in your computer system. However, the system should work for you and not vice versa. You should not evaluate what the system can do first and then design your cost system. Determine what you want the system to do and then evaluate whether the existing or proposed system can accommodate your business needs.

Most cost applications use a very traditional cost accounting model. Anything that is untraditional will require a workaround—tricking the system to make it calculate costs the way you have designed your cost model. Workarounds may result in a unusual setup. At one client, we entered depreciation into the bill of materials because it was the only way we could charge this cost directly to the product. We then modified our accounting procedures to properly classify these costs in the general ledger and developed reports that would segregate costs in the correct categories for management reporting.

Even with workarounds, it may not be possible to implement the design of your cost system given the system limitations. For example, another client has a cost system that calculates fixed overhead as a percent of either labor or materials costs. Their choice is either to calculate the fixed overhead costs outside of the system and enter the cost manually, or to use the overhead cost calculation provided by the system, which may not reflect the true costs of manufacturing. They opted to continue to use the current system, understanding the trade-offs involved with this choice.

Some organizations use a spreadsheet program to develop the costs of their product or services and then enter the unit cost into the appropriate systems application. I strongly discourage this approach. Spreadsheet applications are rarely documented. They are often passed from one employee to another as people leave the organization or change jobs, and the logic behind the original spreadsheet model is often forgotten or not well understood. This situation may result in costing errors or inaccuracies. It also makes it difficult to replicate costs for your products or services based on the information in your system. However, sometimes the nature of the business and the limitations of your costing system may force you to use a database or spreadsheet program for these purposes. If this is the case, make sure that the spreadsheets are properly documented and that they can be tied with relative ease to the unit cost information in the system.

Performance Indicators

A strategic cost system should highlight opportunities to improve the bottom line. Many organizations have performance indicators on yields, occupancy rates, capacity utilization, labor efficiency, customer service levels, and defects per million, but their cost system does not quantify how a change in these measures affects the financial results. As a result, it is often difficult for operations managers to see the link between their actions and the financial performance of the organization. A strategic cost system should have the capability to quantify the financial impact of nonfinancial performance indicators. This calculation may reveal hidden costs and opportunities that are otherwise not visible by analyzing traditional financial reports.

Suppose a pharmaceutical company manufactures two drugs, X and Y. Drug X has a manufacturing yield of 90 percent and Drug Y has a yield of 95 percent. Where should the company focus its improvement efforts—on Drug X or Y? It depends on the sales volumes of the products and the cost of the key ingredient. Suppose Drugs X and Y are both high-volume products. However, the cost of the key ingredient of Drug X is $50 per kilogram and Drug Y, $500 per kilogram. It is possible that when you quantify the financial impact of an improvement in the manufacturing yield for both products, the company would be better off working on Drug Y than Drug X even though it already has a higher manufacturing yield than Drug X. When your cost system can tie nonfinancial performance measures to their cost implications, managers can focus on those areas that will result in higher financial returns for the organization.

A cost system becomes truly valuable when operational managers can understand the financial impact of the decisions that they make on a day-to-day basis in an intuitive manner, without waiting for the month-end financial results. The following anecdote, a true story, illustrates this point. The owner of a company ordered his production supervisor to stop the current production run on a machine and reset the equipment to satisfy a very small order from an important client. This particular machine was very large and had high setup costs. The production supervisor turned to the owner and said something like this: "If you want me to stop the current production run, I will. But it is probably cheaper to buy these units at Kmart and ship them to the customer than to reset this machine for a different product." Production was allowed to continue uninterrupted.

Reports

The sixth element of a cost system is the reporting structure—how information is accessed and presented for decision-making purposes. A strategic cost system should provide users with the capability to generate reports that are simple, understandable, and easy to use. Moreover, users should be able to access this information with minimal intervention from accounting or systems. Unfortunately, many companies do not have these inquiry and reporting capabilities in their information systems. In these situations, reports must be designed and programmed to meet the information needs of the users and allow them to access information in a timely manner.

Accountants typically design the format and content of the cost reports that are distributed to the users. Traditionally, these reports focus on the cost side of the equation only and do not include the critical operational parameters that are driving these costs. A strategic cost system should tie the financial and operational perspective in its reporting structure. It is difficult to understand the costs if you do not understand the context in which those costs were generated. Some key operational parameters may be sales or production volume in units, transaction volume, hours billed, and process or labor hours used, among others. Suppose you were designing a report to show the manufacturing costs of your products. A well-designed report would not only show the cost breakdown by major cost category (e.g., labor, materials, and overhead) but also the key operational parameters driving the costs: labor hours, setup hours, process hours, and manufacturing yield. In this manner, the user can understand the cost differences from one product to another by examining the operational parameters underlying these costs.

Considerations for Effectiveness and Design

Although all cost systems have the six major elements just discussed, some elements are so weak that they diminish the effectiveness of the system as a managerial tool or sometimes even destroy its credibility in the eyes of management. An effective cost system requires that all six elements work in an integrated fashion to provide information that is relevant, timely, and accurate.

You will notice in Figure 2.1 that people are at the center of all six elements. Although I have not included people as an element of a strategic cost system, it is the people who design, operate, and use the system on a day-to-day basis who determine how well it works as a strategic decision-making tool. These people are found in all areas of the organization, from the accountants who record and analyze financial data to the frontline employees who are entering detailed production or customer transactions.

Beyond an integration of the six elements, a cost system should have a well-thought-out design that reflects the management philosophy and has a sound theoretical framework. This design should take into consideration certain key attributes, which, in my experience, are essential to developing a robust system that will withstand the test of time. These attributes are discussed in depth in the next section.

ATTRIBUTES OF A STRATEGIC COST SYSTEM

Strategic cost systems possess certain key attributes that determine their usefulness as a financial and managerial decision-making tool. These seven attributes are listed in Figure 2.2. An understanding of these attributes is fundamental because they will be used to make trade-off decisions that affect your cost system design. By coming back to these key attributes, a project team can justify decisions in terms of how cost data will be gathered, calculated, or reported within a sound theoretical framework.

Figure 2.2 Attributes of a Strategic Cost System

---

1. Cost systems should be simple.
2. Cost systems should be user friendly.
3. Cost systems should be reasonably accurate.
4. Cost systems should be accessible.
5. Cost systems should be flexible and multipurpose.
6. Cost systems should be relevant for decision making.
7. Cost systems should be dynamic.

Key Attribute 1: Cost Systems Should Be Simple

This attribute seems like motherhood and apple pie. Conceptually, we could probably all agree that cost systems should be simple. The implementation of this concept is where the rubber meets the road. Business processes are complex. The challenge is to structure your costing system so that it captures this complexity in a simple manner, understanding the trade-offs that this design might entail.

Many times accounting systems are designed by accountants for accountants. Operations personnel are rarely involved or are only involved on a peripheral basis. The end result is a costing system that, while very accurate, is difficult to understand, explain, or use. One of my clients recently showed me its ABC model for product costing purposes. The system had been originally developed by a cost accounting supervisor who had since been transferred to another division. The accountant who was currently running the costing model understood the mechanics very well, but not the conceptual design. The model had an endless hierarchy of cost allocations, which made it difficult to see how costs flowed to the end product. Because it was only run once a year during the standards-setting process, it had become an accounting tool, not a management information tool, though this was not the intent of the original system design. The complexity of the model and the difficulty in reporting actual costs against the model limited its usefulness for the organization.

Cost systems should be designed so that they capture the business complexity and the process drivers in the simplest manner possible. This attribute is supported by the scientific principle known as *Ockham's razor*. This principle, developed by William of Ockham in the fourteenth century, states that a theory should be as simple as possible to explain a phenomenon. It is highly applicable to the design of strategic cost systems. If trade-offs need to be made between simplicity and accuracy or simplicity and the availability of detailed cost information, it should be a joint decision of the accounting and operations personnel and not an arbitrary decision by one group or another.

Key Attribute 2: Cost Systems Should Be User Friendly

My best analogy for this attribute is Windows versus MS-DOS computer operating systems. For those of you old enough to remember a world before Windows, you will recall that MS-DOS was cumbersome and required the user to invest an enormous amount of time in learning the commands to make the system perform to the user's expectations. Apple Computer's Macintosh and, later, Microsoft's Windows revolutionized the personal computer industry by providing a user interface that was easy to understand and use. *User-friendly* became a mantra for the computer industry and opened up the personal computer to a world beyond the computer "techies."

Cost systems should be easy to understand and use. They should not contain complex accounting jargon or require complex computations that will make it impossible for a user to understand how the information was derived or how to use the information provided. This attribute goes hand-in-hand with simplicity. However, a cost system may be simple and user-unfriendly. Who defines the ease of use is the end customer of the system, not the system designer or the people in charge of running and maintaining the system. A cost system that uses technical jargon that is not defined, explained, or agreed upon by the end users may be difficult to understand and use from their perspective. Some winners in the user-unfriendliness category include terms such as *fully absorbed costs*[4] and *absorption variance.*[5]

Another reason for a user-unfriendly system is the complexity of the costing methodology and the assignment of indirect costs to products and services. Figure 2.3 shows the traditional two-stage allocation model commonly used in many costing systems. Costs are collected by cost centers, departments, or business units. Support departments are usually assigned in some reasonable manner to the business units responsible for manufacturing a product or providing a service. The total costs of these business units are then assigned to the product or service based on some reasonable assignment basis, usually process hours, labor hours, or volume (units, transactions, etc.). In many cost systems, there are so many intermediate layers of cost assignment that it is difficult to analyze costs or use the calculated costs to identify cost improvement opportunities.

User-friendliness may limit the flexibility of the system—how information is gathered, summarized, and reported. A highly flexible cost system may be difficult to understand and use, particularly for nonfinancial managers. Again, I revert back to a systems analogy. UNIX is a highly flexible operating system, but not very user-friendly. Windows, on the other hand,

Figure 2.3 The Traditional Cost Assignment Model

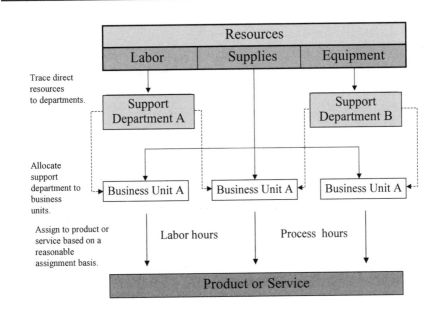

is very user-friendly but has more limited flexibility. User-friendliness and flexibility may often be at odds with each other. Cost system designers should consider the relative importance of this attribute for the organization and make the necessary trade-offs in the system design to meet user requirements.

Key Attribute 3: Cost Systems Should Be Reasonably Accurate

Costs are an *estimate* of the resources used to manufacture the product or service. A cost system should produce unit costs that are reasonably accurate and that differentiate the level of resources required by a product or service without burdening the cost model with too much complexity. The distinction between accuracy and precision is critical. Accuracy involves estimating the true but "unknown" costs. Precision entails estimating costs in excruciating detail. Precision must be balanced against accuracy. More precision does not imply more accuracy. You can be tremendously detailed and precise but terribly incorrect. The difference between precision and accuracy can be demonstrated with a simple example. Suppose you were

Figure 2.4 Precision versus Accuracy

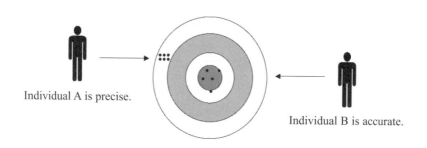

Individual A is precise.

Individual B is accurate.

Which one would you hire as your bodyguard?

hiring a bodyguard and gave two individuals a marksmanship test of shooting at a bull's-eye. Figure 2.4 shows the results of the marksmanship test. Person A is very precise, but totally inaccurate. Person B is accurate, but not as precise. Which one would you rather have as a bodyguard?[6]

Cost systems designers should strive to obtain the highest accuracy possible, even if this sacrifices precision. The cost system designers should determine what level of precision they want in their cost calculations and what trade-offs they are willing to make in terms of complexity and the accuracy of their costs. A greater level of precision usually adds layers of complexity to the cost model as we saw in Figure 2.3. In addition, data gathering and processing have a cost. As cost systems increase in complexity, they become more difficult to maintain and are more prone to errors by the user responsible for updating information.

Key Attribute 4: Cost Systems Should Be Accessible

Cost information should be readily accessible to the key decision makers that must use this information for tactical and strategic decisions. Key management personnel should not only have access to the cost data, but the operational parameters driving the costs. However, a note of caution is in order. Make sure that the key personnel who are using the cost information are properly trained in its use. The use (or misuse) of cost information can steer managers down the wrong path. Ideally, managers should involve their finance experts when using cost information for major management decisions.

Key Attribute 5: Cost Systems Should Be Flexible and Multipurpose

There are different costs for different purposes, depending on the type of situation that is being analyzed. The cost system design should have enough flexibility so that the information can be adapted to different business situations. For example, a breakeven analysis will require the identification of fixed and variable costs. The calculation of the full cost of a product or service will require the identification of direct and indirect costs. An analysis to subcontract services to an outside vendor should only look at the incremental or relevant costs that will be incurred as a result of this decision. Your cost system should be able to handle these different cost views without a problem.[7] It should not be a special project every time you need cost information for a particular purpose.

Key Attribute 6: Cost Systems Should Be Relevant for Decision Making

Although this attribute seems pretty obvious, you would be surprised at how many cost systems I have seen that are not used for management decision making. Usually the accounting system will produce financial reports at month-end that show budget versus actual costs by account or major cost category for the business unit or department. Although managers focus on controlling departmental spending and budget variances, they lack critical information on how process inefficiencies, underutilized resources, and idle capacity affect the bottom line. They often have no idea of the demands that different customers, channels of distribution, products, or services place on their organizational resources and whether these resources could be invested in more profitable endeavors. Some organizations, as a matter of policy, deny key managers access to detailed cost information. This lack of relevant cost information often leads to poor decisions, missed opportunities, and wasted resources.

Key Attribute 7: Cost Systems Should Be Dynamic

Organizations change and evolve and so should your cost system. Many organizations establish a costing methodology and do not update the system setup despite radical changes in the business. Users of cost information should periodically reexamine their cost preparation methods to ensure that these continue to reflect the business of the firm.

In addition, the key operational parameters that underlie the system should be reviewed on an annual basis. The best costing methodology, system applications, accounting procedures, and reporting structure will not compensate for obsolete information. I have had clients—subsidiaries of multinational corporations—who have not updated their time or materials standards in over three years following corporate directives. This situation makes the cost system a mere accumulator of numbers, with no relevance to the business processes that are driving the costs. It is impossible to look for cost improvement opportunities when the information is obsolete.

SUMMARY

We have discussed the six elements that compose a cost system and how these elements interact to produce reliable, accurate, and relevant costs. A strategic cost system requires that all six elements work in harmony and support the management philosophy of the organization. When evaluating your cost system, it is important to assess each element to determine its impact on your ability to provide good cost information. An undue focus on one element such as the costing methodology may result in a system design that is theoretically very sound, but impossible to implement in a cost-effective manner.

In addition, cost systems should be designed with certain key attributes in mind. These seven attributes will ensure the usefulness and longevity of the cost system as the organization evolves over time. An understanding of these key attributes will also allow system designers to make trade-offs as they debate the theoretical underpinnings of the model and their practical implementation in the real world.

ENDNOTES

1. For more information on this survey, see "Roles and Practices in Management Accounting Today," *Strategic Finance* (July 2003): 1–6, and *2003 Survey of Management Accounting* (Ernst & Young, 2003).

2. *Overhead costs* represent the indirect costs of providing a product or service. They typically include indirect labor (i.e., supervisors, maintenance employees), miscellaneous supplies, occupancy, and depreciation, among others.

3. The *bill of materials* contains a list of all components, ingredients, or raw materials and the quantities required of each item to produce a finished product. The item master contains detailed information about all components, subassemblies, and finished products used or manufactured by the organization. The *routing file*, or some similar software application, contains the sequence of operations that will be performed on the product and the detailed labor hours, machine hours, and the setup time that will be required by each operation. These concepts are explained in more detail in Chapter 5.

4. *Fully absorbed costs* are an accounting euphemism for *total costs*. It is the sum of the labor, material, and other costs (also known as overhead) required to manufacture your products or deliver your services. The specific items that are included in the full-cost calculation vary from company to company. For example, some companies include general and administrative costs as part of the product or service cost, while others treat it as an operating expense.

5. *Absorption variance* is recorded by companies that use a standard cost system. The standard cost is the expected cost of the product based on a set of predetermined standards. The difference between the standard and actual cost of a product or service is the absorption variance. A favorable absorption variance means your actual costs were lower than your expected or standard costs; an unfavorable variance means they were higher. From a

decision-making standpoint, variance analysis is not useful unless you delve into the business reasons that created the variance and take actions to reduce that variance in the future. If the variance is permanent, the standard should be revised at the next available opportunity. For more detail on the nature of standard costs and variance analysis, see Lianabel Oliver, *The Cost Management Toolbox: A Manager's Guide to Controlling Costs and Boosting Profits* (New York: AMACOM, 2000), chapter 13.

6. The author would like to acknowledge the contribution of Dr. Ricardo González Méndez, a professor in the Department of Radiological Sciences at the University of Puerto Rico Medical Sciences Campus, in defining the difference between precision and accuracy as explained in this section. He also provided a visual explanation of the concept as shown in Figure 2.4.

7. For a detailed discussion of the different types of costs, see Lianabel Oliver, *The Cost Management Toolbox: A Manager's Guide to Controlling Costs and Boosting Profits* (New York: AMACOM, 2000), chapter 2; or Charles T. Horngren, George Foster, and Srikant M. Datar, *Cost Accounting: A Managerial Emphasis*, 11th ed. (Englewood Cliffs, NJ: Prentice-Hall, Inc., 2003).

3

Redesign Process

In my experience, companies wait too long before embarking on a cost system redesign project. There always seem to be more pressing priorities in the day-to-day operations, and as long as the financial statements are reasonably accurate in the aggregate, line managers learn to live with mediocre cost information. It is only when the cost system results in dysfunctional behaviors or poor business decisions that management becomes highly motivated to make a change.

The implementation of a new cost system is a major organizational undertaking. A successful implementation requires management commitment, careful planning, continuous follow-up, and persistence in the face of adversity. For those of you who have managed major projects in your organizations, the material in this chapter will seem very familiar. A cost redesign project is managed in a similar manner to other projects in your organization. It must have objectives, deliverables, due dates, and accountability. It should have a project leader and team members, each with their assigned areas of responsibility.

In this chapter, we will provide an overview of the cost system redesign process. We will describe the different project stages and how to set up the project to increase its probabilities of success. We will discuss in detail how to organize the project, as this stage is possibly the most critical part of the process.

STAGES OF A COST SYSTEM REDESIGN PROJECT

There are six stages to a cost system redesign project. Each stage involves key decisions and a particular set of tasks that are critical to determining the future direction of the project:

1. Preliminary needs assessment

2. Project organization

3. System design

4. Systems setup and test

5. System implementation

6. Evaluation and review

While the stages follow a sequential order, the redesign process itself is of an iterative nature. As a team acquires more information during the design, development, or implementation process, it may want to go back and revisit prior decisions and agreements. For example, during the development of the costing methodology (a Stage 3 task) a team might want to go back and reexamine some of the project objectives and the deliverables, a Stage 2 task. This continual questioning by team members will result in a more robust cost system that will be accepted and used by the management team.

In the next sections, we will explain the decisions and tasks that should be taken at each stage of the redesign project.

PRELIMINARY NEEDS ASSESSMENT

A preliminary needs assessment is an evaluation of the six elements of a cost system and how well these elements are working together to provide cost information. It allows you to determine the nature and depth of the problem and gives you an idea of the next steps that will be required to address the issues uncovered. It involves interviewing the key users of cost information from different areas, examining the general ledger and financial reports, understanding the current costing methodology, and evaluating the capabilities of your systems applications to gather, store, and report data.

A needs assessment is typically done by one or two individuals. The individual charged with this responsibility should be someone knowledgeable about line operations as well as the accounting systems, processes, and procedures. He or she will prepare a set of findings and recommendations to the management team for further action. Due to resource limitations and the desire for an objective situational analysis, a needs assessment is often performed by outside consultants specializing in cost management.

The needs assessment should define the next steps for the management team, depending on the issues uncovered. A cost system redesign project is only one of many possible solutions, depending on the findings. The problem could be a lack of experienced personnel, the organizational structure, poor communications with line management, or lack of employee training and development. However, if the preliminary needs assessment indicates that a major overhaul of the cost system is required, a cost system redesign effort should be undertaken and a project team organized.

PROJECT ORGANIZATION

The organization of the project is the most critical stage of the redesign process. During this stage, key decisions are made that will affect all other stages of the project. Figure 3.1 shows the recommended steps involved in the organization of a cost redesign project based on my experience. Although the order of these steps may vary depending on the culture and management style of your organization, these tasks are necessary to ensure that the project starts off with the right focus and direction.

Step 1: Get Management Commitment

The most important step in the project organization is obtaining management commitment, not only from top management but also from the middle managers who control the project's resources. A cost system redesign is not an accounting project; it is a strategic initiative that will require the involvement and support of many areas of the organization. If the entire

Figure 3.1 Project Organization

1. Get management commitment.

2. Define the project structure.

3. Develop project plan.

4. Estimate costs.

5. Get management approval.

management team is not committed to the process, the chances of a successful implementation are severely hindered.

The buy-in process usually requires a presentation to management and other key players in the organization on the proposed nature of the project, the key deliverables, the project structure, and the preliminary timetable. This information should be based on the results of the preliminary needs assessment discussed previously. It should be emphasized that this project proposal could be subject to change once the team is assembled and the project is formally defined. If after this presentation the management team is lukewarm on the project or is noncommittal, *do not embark on this initiative.* It will be a waste of time and resources that will not produce the desired results.

Step 2: Define the Project Structure

A cost system redesign project is not a project that can be handled by a lone ranger. It requires the involvement of several key players and the definition of a set of rules that will determine how significant decisions are to be made. There are three major players in a cost redesign project: the steering committee, the facilitator or project manager, and the team members. Their roles and responsibilities are shown in Figure 3.2.

The *steering committee* is the body of individuals that oversees the planning and implementation of the cost redesign system. It is generally composed of the upper management personnel of the site or organizational unit that is undertaking the project. The steering committee reviews and approves the decisions made by the team at key checkpoints in the process. It also allocates additional resources in terms of manpower, equipment, or other types of resources that may be required as the project evolves.

The *project facilitator* provides direction and focus to the project team. This person should be an experienced individual in cost management with a strong background in accounting processes and systems. In addition, he should have project management experience and have a working knowledge of the business operation. This person will be responsible for keeping the project moving according to the established timetable and helping the team clarify theoretical and practical issues that will surface during the design and implementation phases of the project. The project facilitator

Figure 3.2 Suggested Project Structure

Steering Committee
- Approves key decisions
- Assigns resources
- Monitors progress

Project Facilitator
- Provides direction and focus
- Keeps team on track
- Helps team identify and resolve issues

Team Members
- Gather and analyze information
- Develop and implement system design

can be an outside consultant or an internal resource. If the project facilitator is an outside consultant, they should have a *project leader* within the organization, who is also part of the project team and acts as the main point of contact with the rest of the project team on a day-to-day basis. The project leader would assist the outside facilitator in gathering and communicating information to the rest of the team members and may serve as a liaison with members of the steering committee.

If outside consultants are used, the role of the consultant should be defined upfront. Will the consultant be a trainer, a facilitator, a data gatherer, a system designer, or all of the above? The use of consultants is not required for a successful implementation. It depends on the internal resources available within the firm, the level of project management and cost expertise, and the timeframe desired for implementation.

The *project team* performs the actual design and implementation of the system. Members serve on a full- or part-time basis. The amount of time that team members can devote to the project will affect the implementation timetable. In my experience, team members work on the cost system redesign in addition to their day-to-day responsibilities. It can consume anywhere from 10 to 25 percent of their available work hours and, at key points in the process, may require 100 percent dedication by some team members. The project team should be cross-functional and include at least one representative from the following areas: business operations, accounting, and information systems. In a manufacturing setting, it would probably include a production manager, a cost analyst, a materials planner or buyer, an industrial engineer, and a programmer analyst. In a service setting such as a financial services institution, it would probably have a similar composition substituting the production manager for an expert in retail banking and ensuring that the industrial engineer is familiar with banking operations, particularly transaction processing. Within this project structure, one of these individuals would act as project leader and would also undertake the project facilitation, if an external resource is not used for this purpose. The criteria for assignment to the project team should include the following:

○ Familiarity with the company processes and products
○ Level of credibility with the organization
○ Level of expertise in the functional area
○ Time available for the project

You want the best and the brightest on your project team. You do not assign these tasks to your poor performers!

As part of project structure, the team should define the frequency of how often they will meet and for how long. I strongly recommend setting aside three or four hours on a fixed day of the week so that team members can block their calendars and reserve this time to work on the project. Meetings can be weekly, biweekly, or monthly depending on the implementation timeframe. The meetings should be a time to discuss conceptual issues, identify possible roadblocks, and review and communicate information. Team members will be required to work outside of the meeting in their particular areas of expertise and present the results to the team for discussion. The project facilitator should document team meetings by preparing minutes that are published after the meeting. The minutes should summarize the discussions and any key decisions or agreements that were made during the meeting. The minutes serve a dual purpose. One, they document the work of the team and provide written evidence of discussions that can be used to clarify or refresh a particular issue in the future. Two, they provide a communication vehicle to the steering committee and other interested parties in terms of the project status and progress.

Finally, team members should define the communication and approval process for key decisions at each stage of the project. What types of decisions need approval by the steering committee? What will be the frequency of the checkpoints? Who else needs to be involved? What type of information do they need, and at what level of detail? The definition of the communication and approval process is vital to ensure that major decisions are not reversed at a critical stage of the project. Once this process is defined, it should be presented to the steering committee as part of the overall project plan.

Step 3: Develop Project Plan

Once the project team has been assembled, its first priority is to develop a project plan for approval by the steering committee. The project plan should include the following information:

○ *A description of the business needs.* The business needs describe the organizational requirements for its new cost system. It should be based on the preliminary needs assessment and should be validated by the project team. It should describe the key attributes of the new system and what information it should provide to the user community.

○ *A statement of project objectives.* The project objectives should clearly define the intent of the new cost system in terms of what information will be provided and how the information will be used. For example, the cost system could be designed with an *external focus* attempting to understand product or customer profitability and thereby impact the sales and marketing strategies of the organization; however, it could have an *internal focus* identifying the resources consumed by the product or service to uncover cost reduction opportunities and process efficiencies. A cost system could have multiple purposes, having both an internal and external focus and providing different types of cost information for decision-making purposes. A cost system that has multiple purposes will probably have a greater degree of complexity and take longer to implement than one with a single purpose in mind.

○ *A definition of the project scope.* The scope sets the project boundaries. It will determine the time and effort required to complete the project. Here are some factors to consider:

- *The number of organizational units.* The scope defines the number of organizational units that will be analyzed as part of the project. If the organization has multiple sites or service facilities, the scope can be limited to one site or to specific business units within a site.

- *Nature and number of items to be costed.* What is the nature of the items to be costed—are they products, services, customers, geographic regions, business units, business processes, or all of the above? Which items do you want to cost in detail? The number and diversity of items will affect the data gathering and analysis process as well as implementation timetable.

- *System applications.* This factor sets boundaries on the system applications. Will the team be given the flexibility to explore a change in its system applications to improve the access and availability of information, or is the team limited to the constraints imposed by the current systems environment? Will stand-alone databases be allowed, or should all required information be entered into the main systems applications? Although a cost system should not be driven by the current systems applications, system limitations can add to the complexity of the implementation or require certain trade-offs in the design process. The team should understand any system limitations upfront as part of defining the project scope.

○ *A list of key deliverables.* This section should detail the expected outputs of the project in terms of information, procedures, and documentation. For example, an expected result of this type of project would be the development and documentation of a new cost methodology that satisfies the project objectives. The list of key deliverables may change or evolve as the project progresses. This list is a first step that will be used to direct and focus the team during the design and implementation process.

○ *Development of the project schedule.* The project timetable details the tasks involved in the design and implementation process. It defines the major milestones, identifies the tasks to be accomplished, assigns responsibility for each task listed, and sets due dates. The time required to implement a new cost system is highly dependent on the scope of the project and the resources assigned. For example, the development of a new cost methodology may take between four to six months using part-time resources. With full-time resources, this timetable can be significantly shorter. In my experience, companies are far too aggressive in their time estimates, given the resources that they are willing to devote to the project. This situation may cause the project to fall behind schedule. There are also others factors that can affect the project schedule:

- *Experience and expertise of the team.* A team that has highly experienced personnel will work faster and more effectively because they know the ins and outs of the organization and how to find and access information.

- *Changing project requirements.* If management shifts the requirements of the project mid-stream, it will affect the ability of the team to meet their objectives. Therefore, it is very important to have checkpoints with the steering committee after the completion of each major milestone to avoid rework after the system design has been completed or—even worse—implemented.

- *Shifting priorities.* Day-to-day responsibilities can overwhelm team members and limit the time they have available to work on the project. This issue may become particularly problematic if the immediate supervisor of the team member has not bought into the project. If shifting priorities are creating a problem for a particular team member or for the team as a whole, it is important to bring this situation to the attention of the steering committee and re-set priorities according to the needs of the organization.

Figure 3.3 Elements of the Project Plan
_____

- Description of the business needs
- Statement of project objectives
- Definition of the project scope
- List of key deliverables
- Preliminary project schedule

Figure 3.3 summarizes the elements that should be included in the project plan. My advice to team members is as follows: Be conservative in setting the project schedule. Usually, when someone tells me two weeks, it takes four. Be sure to consider other important events that may be due around the same time as your task completion dates or project milestones such as year-end close, budgeting, regulatory inspections, audits, and corporate visits, among others. No one will penalize you for finishing a task early, but it might reflect poorly on the team if it falls significantly behind schedule.

Step 4: Estimate Costs

After the project plan is completed and documented, the next step is to develop cost estimates based on the project plan. A cost system redesign project can be a costly investment. The team can estimate the cost of the project, on an incremental or a full cost basis. Incremental costs only consider the additional cash outlays that the company will incur as a result of the project. Typical incremental costs may include consultant fees, training seminars, books, software, or equipment. Full costs would include all costs incurred by the project including a portion of the salary and fringe benefits of the team members based on the percent of time that they are dedicated to the project.

Some companies may require a return on investment calculation such as the payback period or net present value as part of the cost-benefit analysis. This type of calculation will require making assumptions as to the potential cost savings or incremental revenue that can be obtained as a result of having better information. In my experience, cost estimates usually only identify the incremental costs of the project. Managers are mainly concerned about whether the costs have been budgeted or whether they can be spent without incurring a budget overrun. The team members may wish to prepare for this eventuality as part of the process of obtaining final management approval for the project.

Step 5: Get Management Approval

This step represents the completion of a major milestone—the formal approval of the project. It usually involves a presentation of the project plan, structure, and timetable to top management and any other key managers that will be affected by the project. This step has a twofold purpose: (1) it will reaffirm the management commitment obtained in Step 1 and (2) it will allow management an opportunity to revisit the project plan that has been formally assembled by the team. At this point, the steering committee may decide to make changes in terms of requirements, scope, or resources based on the organizational priorities. Once the project receives the blessing of the management team, it is ready to proceed to the next stage–the conceptualization of the system design.

SYSTEM DESIGN

In this stage of the project, the team conceptualizes the design of the new cost system, determines what information will be required, and establishes how this information will be captured. The primary focus of the team will be on three elements: the costing methodology, the financial and operational data, and the systems applications. The other elements—procedures, reports, and performance metrics—will be touched tangentially, but will not be fully developed at the completion of this stage. For example, the key cost drivers identified during the development of the cost methodology will usually become the basis of a performance measurement system later on. The team must also ensure that accounting and operational procedures can capture the data required by the cost system without placing an undue burden on the organization. Therefore, these issues must be considered during the design process; the detailed procedures, reporting, or metrics will be addressed at a later point in time. The development of the costing methodology and the system design issues are discussed in detail in Chapters 4 and 6. Therefore, we will defer further discussion of this stage until then.

SYSTEMS SETUP AND TEST

Once the preliminary systems design is agreed upon, the team is ready to start building the cost model. This stage involves four steps:

1. *Data gathering.* The first step involves gathering the financial and operational data that will underlie the model *according to the system design.* A company may have time standards, but the methodology used to develop these standards may not be consistent with the system design. In this situation, the standards will have to be revised to conform to the new methodology. In addition, general ledger information may have to be recast in a different format or procedures put in place to gather operational data that is currently not being collected.

2. *Data validation.* Once the data have been gathered, the team should validate the data for reasonableness. This validation can be done in several ways: by comparing it with actual, budgeted or prior year's data, by reviewing it with experts, or by comparing it to industry or company benchmarks. The validation process will highlight inconsistencies or areas that require further investigation. It will ensure that your cost information is reasonably accurate and representative of the underlying business processes or resources consumed by these processes.

3. *Systems setup.* This step involves setting up your systems application and entering the required data into the system. Most manufacturing companies have an accounting system with some type of costing application that calculates unit costs. Service organizations may be more limited in terms of costing applications and may have to run their costs on a spreadsheet application or purchase a stand-alone system. No matter which system application is used, it should reflect the costing methodology agreed upon in the prior

stage. If the system cannot accommodate the established methodology, then the team should explore if a workaround is possible. If not, the team might have to consider (a) the possibility of costing outside the systems application or (b) changing the design to accommodate the limitations of the system. If the team opts to change the system design, it should understand the trade-offs that it is making in terms of the accuracy and reliability of the cost calculation and document these trade-offs accordingly.

4. *Systems test.* After the system is set up and all data have been entered, the team performs a preliminary cost run and reviews the results. In my experience, this review always results in changes. Usually, there are changes to the setup of the systems application or correction of errors in the financial or operational data. Less frequently, a design change is called for. The team should consider the systems test as an experimentation phase, where they will evaluate whether the output of the system is reasonably accurate and meets the project objectives defined by the team. Again, many cost runs may be required before the system is ready to move into the implementation phase.

During the system setup and testing process, the team may decide to go back and change the system design. Once real data are incorporated into the model, something might not quite work the way the team expected it to. At one manufacturing client, we had decided to distribute support costs to the product using the number of lots produced. When we entered this information into the system, we realized that products that were both manufactured and packaged at the facility would be double-charged for these services—once at the manufacturing stage and another at the packaging stage. We subsequently altered the system design so that product support costs would be assigned only at the manufacturing level. Systems setup and test will be discussed in more detail in Chapter 7.

SYSTEM IMPLEMENTATION

After the system has been thoroughly tested, the project moves into the implementation stage. Depending on the scope of the project, a cost system may be implemented all at once or in a phased approach. For example, you might decide to run a pilot with "live" data in one department or organizational unit before rolling out the new cost system to the rest of the organization. At one of my clients, we developed the cost methodology first and implemented it for the revised 2003 budget. The project team's next steps were to develop the operational and accounting procedures to capture and report actual data and develop metrics that tie the key performance indicators such as capacity and labor utilization to costs. These aspects of the system were tested and documented in the latter part of 2002 for implementation in 2003 when the new cost standards came into effect.

The system implementation will also depend on the project timetable and unavoidable project delays such as management turnover that may defer the scheduled completion date. The optimal implementation date is always the start of a new fiscal year, because in that way the company can start the year "clean" from an accounting standpoint. There are no major upheavals to the financial reporting structure mid-year or no messy explanations of cost variances as a result of the new system. This situation presumes that the budget for that fiscal year was based on the new costing methodology and system redesign. While I do not recommend a mid-year implementation, there are times when it is unavoidable. In these situations, I recommend the system be implemented at the cut-off of an accounting period, preferably at the end of a quarter or the first half of the year. Typically, the company accountants will have to restate the current year financial statements to ensure comparability with prior accounting periods.

During the implementation process, hope for the best, prepare for the worst—Murphy lives! This is not the time for team members to be going on vacation, taking extended business trips, or tackling new assignments. The team members must be ready to react, troubleshoot, and resolve problems so that the business operations can continue with minimal, if any, disruption.

EVALUATION AND REVIEW

During the first year of implementation, the cost system should be reviewed every three to six months to ensure that key objectives are being met and line management is satisfied with the information that is being produced. Once the system is stable, it should be reviewed periodically, particularly if there is a major change in top management, business processes, or the organizational structure (i.e., a merger or acquisition). Other situations may also call for a reexamination of the cost system as discussed in Chapter 2. Cost systems are dynamic; they should evolve and change over time. However, any significant changes to an element of the cost system should be discussed and agreed upon with the users of the cost information. They should not be arbitrary decisions made by a finance manager or a member of her team.

What will be the longevity of your redesigned cost system? My experience tends to indicate that a cost system can usually last from three to five years with no major modifications. This longevity does not imply that it remains static, but that it grows and evolves with changes in the business.

SUMMARY

In this chapter, we described the six stages of a cost system redesign project: (1) the preliminary needs assessment, (2) the project organization, (3) the system design, (4) the system setup and test, (5) the implementation, and (6) the evaluation and review. Each stage involves key decisions and a particular set of tasks that are critical to ensure the project success. The project organization is the most critical stage of the project because key decisions are made that will affect all other stages.

While cost redesign projects generally follow through the stages in a sequential order, team members should feel free to question any issue or decision made in a prior stage. Just because an issue was decided in a prior stage does not mean it cannot be reexamined at a later date, particularly if new facts or information call for a reassessment of the decision. This type of group dynamics will result in a more robust cost system.

In Chapters 4 and 5, we will delve into the details of the cost system design and the issues that should be addressed during this process.

4

Conceptualizing the Cost Model Design

After the project plan has been approved, the first order of business is to conceptualize the overall system design. The system design defines the theoretical framework that will underlie the cost system and how it will be applied in your company. It requires an understanding of the business processes and a determination of how the resource consumption by these processes will be captured in your costs. During this stage, specific issues should be addressed, and specific tasks should be completed. The failure to address these issues and tasks upfront may result in a cost model that is too complex or cannot be implemented due to internal or external constraints.

Cost systems are a continuous work in progress. Although the design stage lays the foundation and provides direction for the subsequent phases of the project, the system will evolve as the project progresses or in response to the changing business environment. Therefore, as the team gains more information and experience, it may decide to revisit decisions made at this stage. In this chapter, we will discuss the major milestones and tasks that should be accomplished during the design stage. The completion of these milestones will ensure consistency in the data collection process and minimize wasted time and effort in analyzing extraneous information.

MAJOR MILESTONES

There are two major milestones during the system design stage: (1) the definition of key terms that will underlie the theoretical framework and (2) the development of the preliminary costing methodology that will be used to calculate unit costs. The definition of key terms is critical because how a particular item is defined may affect how time standards will be set or how the costs will be calculated. For example, the term "standard costs" could be defined as follows:

> *Standard costs* are the sum of the labor, materials, and overhead costs required to produce a product using the process specifications under *normal* operating conditions. Overheads costs include all support areas such as such as planning, purchasing, maintenance, quality control, engineering, accounting, human resources, and information systems.

However, standard costs could also be defined in the following manner:

> *Standard costs* are the sum of the labor, materials, and overhead costs required to produce a product using the process specifications under *efficient* operating conditions. Overheads costs include indirect manufacturing support areas such as planning, purchasing, maintenance, quality control, and engineering, but exclude the cost of general and administrative areas such as accounting, human resources, and information systems.

While both definitions are correct, their costing implications are very different. The development of costs using process specifications under normal operating conditions may result in process inefficiencies being included in the standard. In addition, under the first definition, the standard cost would include all costs of manufacturing a product; in the second definition, the general and administrative costs would be excluded from the cost calculation.

Although there are standard definitions in the accounting and operational literature, the team should decide what definition is appropriate for its business and ensure that it is acceptable to the steering committee overseeing the project. Key definitions should include both accounting and operational terms. For example, what is the definition of process time? What activities characterize the start and end of a particular process? What is considered setup time? What type of allowances will be made for employee fatigue and equipment reliability? In my experience, the process of agreeing on a set of definitions will make for lively discussions among the team members. In service organizations, this process may present special challenges because some terms commonly used in manufacturing organizations (such as *setup* or *yield*) are not widely used in service. Their lack of use does not mean the concept is not applicable to these organizations. However, reaching agreement on the applicability of these concepts and how they will be used in the costing structure may take more time and effort than in a manufacturing setting, where individuals are more familiar with their use. The agreement of the key terms and definitions sets the theoretical underpinnings of the costing methodology. Appendix A provides an example of key terms and definitions, which can be used as a starting point for any cost redesign project.

The second major milestone is the development of the *preliminary* costing methodology. I emphasize the word *preliminary* because it might change during the course of the project. The costing methodology describes how unit costs will be calculated. It will define what costs will be included or excluded from the calculation and the reasons for this determination. It will explain how indirect costs or overhead will be assigned to products or services and will identify the most appropriate assignment basis. In the next section, we will discuss in more detail how to develop the costing methodology and identify the issues that should be addressed and resolved as part of this process.

COSTING METHODOLOGY

A good cost system should reflect the resources the organization is spending on its processes, products, services, or customers. The costing methodology is the detailed procedure that explains how the organization will calculate these costs. It is based on the key terms and definitions agreed upon by the team, and its design requires a thorough understanding of the business and accounting processes. Even at this early stage, you do not want to design a costing methodology that will place an undue burden on the organization in terms of data collection or reporting. In this section, I have outlined the major steps that a team should take in developing its costing methodology. These steps are summarized in Figure 4.1. Although I have placed them in sequential order, I would like to emphasize that this is not a sequential process. These steps may be carried out in parallel or in a different order without affecting the desired results.

Figure 4.1 Steps in the Development of the Costing Methodology

1. Identify the cost objects.

2. Identify the specific information deliverables.

3. Understand the business processes.

4. Determine the cost basis.

5. Understand the cost structure.

6. Agree on a preliminary costing methodology.

Step 1: Identify the Cost Objects

The first step in the development of the methodology is the identification of the *cost objects*—the items that are to be measured or costed. For most companies, the primary cost objects will be the products and services delivered to intermediate or end customers. Though the cost objects are identified in the project scope in general terms, once the team starts evaluating the cost methodology it must focus on specific items or groups of items. For companies with many diverse products and services, costing 100 percent of all items is probably not a realistic target. This universe of possibilities needs to be narrowed down to manageable proportions. Even if a company has a limited number of items, resource constraints may not permit the team to examine each item in detail. For example, at one of my clients, the project team concentrated its efforts on eight major product families. Though the company manufactured other products, we felt that these did not have a significant impact on the costs or the business operations and therefore, the costs of these products could be estimated based on the resource consumption of similar products.

Step 2: Identify the Specific Information Deliverables

Next, the team should understand what information the cost system is expected to provide based on the project objectives and the implications it may have for the costing methodology. For example, if you want to report the costs of excess capacity, you will need to define what constitutes practical or available capacity, and perform a unit cost calculation based on this information. If fact, this requirement might lead you to have two costs: one with excess capacity buried in the product costs (the *full cost absorption* that accountants love) and another based on practical or available capacity, which excludes the costs of excess capacity in the cost calculations.[1] Full cost absorption and the treatment of excess or idle capacity will be explained in more detail in Chapter 6, which covers costing issues.

Another example is the level of cost detail that management requires for decision-making or reporting purposes. A company may decide that the unit cost of the product or service is sufficient without having to break it down into its individual cost components such as labor, materials, and overhead. Another company may decide that it not only requires this minimum level of detail, but would like to see the costs of any intermediate products or services broken down by major cost category as well. It is important to define the requirements upfront at this point to ensure that the costing methodology will enable you to provide the necessary information to manage the business on a day-to-day basis without recurring to special analyses or manual spreadsheets to access and report the information.

Step 3: Understand the Business Processes

The costing methodology requires a solid understanding of the business processes. Since all team members will not have the same level of knowledge of the business operations, the first order of business is to educate the team on how the key processes are run. My experience is that even team representatives from the operations area are sometimes surprised by what they uncover during this analysis. The objective of this exercise is to obtain as much information as possible on the products or services provided. Here are some questions to ask:

- What is the nature of the products or services?
- How are they produced and delivered?
- What are the key business processes involved?
- What types of resources do these products or services require?

○ Do they require dedicated equipment or specialized personnel?

○ Do they place significant requirements on support areas such as customer service, quality control, purchasing, engineering, information systems, or accounting?

If your organization has implemented process improvements programs such as Six Sigma, total quality management, or reengineering,[2] this information might already be available in your organization. The team should determine what information is available that would be useful for understanding the business processes. Some examples include engineering studies, consultants' reports, and process flowcharts. The team might also have to meet with process experts or task specialists to clarify information or questions that may arise during the course of this fact-finding mission.

Team members should also observe the business operations and talk to the employees actually involved in the production or service-delivery process. During this tour, team members may uncover information that is not documented anywhere or that will make a difference in how products or services should be costed. One critical piece of information is to determine the nature of the process. Is it labor-driven, machine-driven, or customer-driven? In a labor-driven operation, the employees determine the rate of output. For example, the apparel industry has traditionally been a very labor-intensive operation. In machine-driven processes, the equipment sets the pace of service or production. For example, in a medical clinic that provides radiological services, an X-ray machine has a standard process time per X-ray, which will determine the maximum number of X-rays that can be taken during any given time period. In customer-driven processes, the customer sets the pace of output. An example of this type of process would be self-checkout registers or ATM machines where the customer is an integral part of service delivery process. Some processes are hybrid operations. While the equipment operates at a predetermined rate, the interaction of the employees with the equipment can significantly affect the time required to complete the operation or the output obtained. Once the team understands the business processes, it is in a better position to analyze costs.

Step 4: Determine the Cost Basis

In this step, the team will decide what type of costs will be used to set up and test the cost model. This decision should be made before analyzing the cost structure of the organization. The team may use actual costs, budgeted costs, or recast cost information. Recast cost information starts from a base point such as the annual budget and adjusts the costs for specific situations, such as a restructuring of the business process or the elimination of the depreciation expense of idle equipment. The type of cost information chosen will determine the financial information that must be gathered in order to analyze the cost structure. The team must be consistent between the choice of costs and the operational information that underlies these costs. If you choose to use budgeted costs, then you must use budgeted operational data in your cost calculations and analysis (i.e., labor and process times, production or service volumes, etc.). If not, your cost model will not provide an accurate representation of the cost structure because there is an inconsistency between the cost information and the operational data that underlie the cost calculations. If your team chooses to use actual costs, you must ensure that the time periods for gathering the financial and operational information are consistent. For example, you should not calculate a cost based on the financial information of a six-month period ending in June and the operational data of a six-month period ending in August. This methodology is not internally consistent and will probably result in inaccurate costs. The degree of inaccuracy will depend on the monthly or seasonal fluctuations in the financial and operational data.

Step 5: Understand the Cost Structure

The nature of the business processes usually drives the costs of an organization. However, sometimes there is a disassociation between how the business is run and how the costs are collected and reported. A key activity of the project team is to relate the business processes to the costs incurred by the organization. An analysis of the cost structure involves the following:

○ Identification of the most significant costs for the organization

○ Determination of their cost behavior pattern

○ Traceability of costs to the items produced or services delivered
○ Identification of the key cost drivers

A examination of the financial statements and reports will allow the team to identify the most significant costs of the organization as a whole and the breakdown of these costs by business process or functional area. The team should start at an aggregate level and work its way down to the detail. The income statement is an excellent starting point, because it will show the most significant costs of the organization broken down by major cost category. In manufacturing organizations, the most significant costs will often be found in labor, materials, and overhead, whereas in service organizations, labor, depreciation, and facilities constitute the most significant cost categories. A good understanding of what percent these items represent of the total organizational cost structure will focus the team on where to concentrate its efforts. For example, if you discover that overhead represents only 2 to 4 percent of your total product costs, you may not want to spend much time in the overhead allocation methodology and would certainly not want to implement an activity-based costing system.[3]

Once the key business processes have been identified, the team might want to delve into the cost structure of these specific processes. Accounting systems usually capture costs according to the departmental structure of the organization. Therefore, the general ledger might not be structured to provide the team with cost information for its key processes. In this situation, the financial information will have to be recast to provide the data in a meaningful format for the team. This recasting of financial data is a nontrivial exercise. However, it may be critical to get a solid handle on the cost structure of the organization.

The team should then proceed to examine the cost behavior patterns of these costs and their traceability to the cost objects. This understanding can have a significant influence on the costing methodology. An analysis of cost behavior patterns will show how costs behave with changes in volume. Which costs are fixed? Which are variable? Sometimes, the accounting system may classify a cost as variable when, in fact, it is a semivariable or fixed cost. For example, in the pharmaceutical industry, some companies have manufacturing operations that require a minimum of two production operators regardless of whether they produce one lot or one thousand lots per year. In this type of situation, the labor costs should be considered fixed because they will not vary according to the volume produced. The cost accounting system, however, will probably classify them as a variable cost because traditional accounting systems consider direct labor as a variable cost. It is sometimes difficult for accountants to break this traditional mode of thinking to reflect what is really happening on the manufacturing floor or in the service facility.

The cost behavior pattern may also determine how the particular cost category will be set up in the system. Variable costs, such as labor and materials, will change in direct proportion to the amount of material or labor consumed by the product or service. They can usually be traced specifically to a product or service. Semivariable and fixed costs, however, are typically common to more than one product or service. These costs are classified as indirect or overhead costs and are grouped in one or more cost pools for costing purposes.

This discussion brings us to the issue of traceability. Many costs such as electricity, support labor, repair, and maintenance cannot be traced to a specific product or service. These costs are grouped into *cost* or *overhead pools*, which are then distributed to the cost object in some reasonable manner.[4] In an ideal world, you would want all costs to be directly traceable to the product or service, eliminating the need for cost allocations. Once you start allocating costs, you enter an element of inaccuracy into the costing process because even the best allocation basis will not reflect the true resource consumption for the products or services.

Some costs that have been classified traditionally as indirect costs can be converted into direct costs by simply performing a more detailed analysis of the process and its associated costs. One example of this type of cost is depreciation. In traditional cost accounting systems, the depreciation expense is included as part of the fixed overhead pool and is distributed to all products based on labor or process hours. However, if a business unit has equipment that is dedicated to a particular product family or service offering, the depreciation associated with this equipment, as well as any other maintenance and support costs, should be charged only to those products or services. If you include the costs of dedicated equipment in the overhead pool, the cost of the products that use this equipment will be understated and those that do not use the equipment will be overstated.

This costing inaccuracy can affect sales and marketing strategies, pricing, and other management decisions involving these products.

Another type of cost that has traditionally been viewed as indirect is quality control. In many organizations, particularly in regulated industries such as food processing or pharmaceuticals, an established set of tests and procedures must be performed for each product. If all products or services consume the same amount of quality control resources, then these costs can be included in the overhead rate without creating any cost distortion. However, if the products and services require different types of tests that have different process times, then product costs would be misrepresented by including quality control as part of the overhead allocation. If the cost of the quality control function is significant, then the team should evaluate whether to include it as a direct cost of the product or as part of the overhead allocation.

How could you convert the quality control costs from an indirect to direct cost? One possible way is to identify the type of tests that are done for each product, develop time standards for each type of test, and calculate a cost per test in the same manner as you would calculate a cost per product. This cost per test would be used to assign the quality control costs directly to the product based on the number of tests required per unit or per production lot. Another alternative would be to establish standard test hours, expressed as a function of labor or process times, and charge the products based on the number of hours consumed.

The inclusion of the quality control or test function as a direct cost would primarily be applicable to industries where these costs represent a major portion of the total costs of the operation. At one of my clients, the quality control lab represented 6 percent of the total labor and overhead costs of the facility; at another, it was about 11 percent. In both situations, the project teams decided to charge the costs of the quality control function directly to the product or areas that consumed their services because the consumption of this resource varied significantly by product or product family. This decision uncovered several opportunities for cost improvement because it forced the team to analyze the business processes of the quality control function. In both organizations, these areas ceased to be "black holes" and process improvements resulted in a more efficient use of the resources of these departments with a subsequent reduction in costs.

A final activity in understanding the cost structure is the identification of the cost drivers of the key business processes.[5] Here is where the team meshes the operational knowledge gathered in Step 3 with the cost analysis performed in Step 5. The identification of the cost drivers will allow the team to identify where the true areas of cost improvement opportunities may lie. Here are some key questions to ask:

- What causes costs to be incurred in these operations?

- Are they controllable by the organization? (For example, in highly regulated industries, the requirements of regulatory agencies are a significant cost driver of some processes.)

- Given these cost drivers and the nature of the business processes, what would be an appropriate activity measure to distribute indirect costs?

After the team has analyzed the cost structure and related it to the key business processes, it is ready to start developing the preliminary costing methodology.

Step 6: Agree on a Preliminary Costing Methodology

In this step, the team designs a preliminary cost model that will be used in the system setup and testing stage. At this point, it should consider several elements based on the information gathered in the prior steps:

- Which costs are variable? Which are fixed? How will the team treat semivariable costs in the cost model?

- Which costs will be charged directly to the product or service?

- Are there costs that are currently classified as indirect costs that should be charged to a particular product or service?

- Which costs will be considered indirect? How will we group them for overhead allocation purposes?

- Are there costs that should be excluded from the overhead pool (i.e., the cost of excess capacity)?

○ What are the most appropriate measures to assign indirect costs to the cost object?

○ How will yield and scrap be captured in the cost calculation? How will it be reported?

A number of costing issues also need to be discussed and resolved by the project team at this stage. These issues will be discussed in detail in Chapter 6.

After careful consideration of the costing elements and issues, the team should agree on a preliminary methodology that will be used to develop costs. This methodology should describe the cost basis, the major cost components and how these will be calculated, the cost classification (variable-fixed, direct-indirect), and the allocation basis for assigning indirect costs. This preliminary cost model constitutes the completion of a major milestone and should be presented to the steering committee for approval before proceeding to the system setup and test stage.

SUMMARY

The system design stage lays the groundwork for the subquent stages of the project. During this stage, team members will acquire knowledge of the products, services, and business processes and relate these to the costs incurred by the organization. They will use this knowledge to develop a preliminary costing methodology in accordance with the project objectives that reflects the resource consumption of their primary products and services.

The system design phase is an opportunity for the team members to share information and broaden their understanding of the organization. It is a time to debate thorny issues and reach a consensus solution. Members should feel free to raise issues even though they have already been discussed and agreed upon by the team. In my experience, when team members raise concerns, they usually have a valid theoretical, procedural, or operational reason to support their position.

The design of the cost model requires an understanding of the major cost components of the organization and how these are added together to determine the cost of a product or service. We will discuss the traditional cost components of labor, materials, and overhead and how they are typically calculated. The next chapter is included for the benefit of those readers that are unfamiliar with costing practices. If you are experienced in this area, you may choose to skim this chapter.

ENDNOTES

1. For the definitions of practical and available capacity, see Chapter 7 on costing issues.
2. These are different approaches to process improvement. Each approach has a distinct management philosophy and uses statistical and analytical techniques to achieve the desired results. For more information, see Peter S. Pande, Robert P. Nueman, Roland R. Cavanagh, *The Six Sigma Way, How GE, Motorola, and Other Top Companies Are Honing Their Performance* (New York: McGraw-Hill, 2000); Michael Hammer and James Champy, *Reengineering the Corporation* (New York: HarperCollins Publishers, 1993); Phillip Crosby, *Quality is Free: The Art of Making Quality Certain* (New York: Penguin Books, 1979); and *Quality Without Tears: The Art of Hassle-Free Management* (New York: McGraw-Hill, 1984).
3. *Activity-based costing* is a cost management approach that identifies the processes or "activities" involved in supplying a product or service and those resources that these processes consume. It then distributes labor and overhead costs based on intensity or frequency with which the product or service consumes the activity.
4. *Cost pools* are groups of costs that are typically used to distribute indirect costs to products or services. A cost pool can be very broad and can include many cost categories. For example, a company could have a cost pool called facilities, which would include all the costs of repairing and maintaining the production or service facilities. A cost pool can also be very narrow, such as company telecommunications expense. When a company has broad cost pools that encompass many functions and include many different types of cost, the unit cost calculations tend to be less accurate because the method of distributing the costs to

the product or service may not reflect the actual resource consumption.

5. *Cost drivers* are the structural causes of the cost of an activity and differ in the extent to which they can be controlled by the firm. Examples of cost drivers include product or process design, customer specifications, corporate requirements, or government regulations.

5

How to Calculate Costs

In order to design a cost system, team members should have a basic understanding of how costs are put together. The costing methodology describes how an organization calculates its product, service, or customer costs. It can range from very simple to very complex, depending on the size of the organization, the number of items being costed, the complexity of the business processes, and the management philosophy toward cost management. Generally, costs can be divided into three major components: labor, materials, and overhead. The significance of each cost component relative to total costs will vary from industry to industry. For example, in a pure service organization like an accounting firm, materials costs are considerably lower than labor or overhead costs. In manufacturing organizations, on the other hand, materials costs generally represent a significant portion of total production costs.

In this chapter we will discuss the traditional cost components—labor, materials, and overhead—and how they are rolled up into the cost of a product or service. The team may decide to separate a cost component if it is significant enough to merit reporting separately from other costs. For example, if utilities represent a major cost for your organization, the team may decide to report this cost as a separate cost component versus including it as part of overhead costs, as dictated by traditional cost accounting practices.

If you are familiar with costing process, you may wish to skim this chapter. However, understanding the major cost components and how they are assembled is a basic building block of any cost system and one of the starting points for a cost system redesign project.

MATERIALS COSTS

Materials costs are usually significant in those industries that have conversion processes. Conversion processes transform materials through the use of equipment and labor into a useful product or service. Although usually found in manufacturing-related industries, some types of service industries such as power generation or food service also have conversion processes.

Materials Quantity Standards

Materials cost are generally based on materials quantity standards that are described in the *bill of materials (BOM)* or *product structure.* The BOM shows how the product is assembled or manufactured from a materials standpoint. It contains a list of all components, ingredients, or raw materials and the quantities required of each item to produce a finished product. Most organizations that are involved in conversion processes have some type of bill of materials, even if it only consists of a list of components and quantities on a spreadsheet program. Figure 5.1 shows the bill of materials for Product 3902, a bottle of 100 tablets of Multi-A, a generic vitamin tablet. We will use this example to show how materials costs are calculated for a particular product.

Figure 5.1 Sample Bill of Materials for Product 3902

Product Number: **3902**

Description: **Multi-A 100-tablet bottle**

Item Number	Description	Unit of Measure	Quantity per Bottle
3902-01	Multi-A tablets	per thousand	0.10
346256	White plastic bottle	ea	1.02
238902	Cap plastic metal	ea	1.02
LF3902	Front label	ea	1.05
LB3902	Back label	ea	1.05
D00001	Dessicant	ea	1.04
CX1236	Circular	ea	1.04

In examining Figure 5.1, we notice that one 100-tablet bottle of Multi-A vitamins consists of several material components (i.e., a bottle, a plastic cap, etc.) and an intermediate product, which is a tablet of Multi-A vitamin. In manufacturing jargon, this intermediate product is called a *subassembly*. Generally, subassemblies are used to manufacture another product and are not sold to end customers; they are produced for internal consumption only. A subassembly also has a bill of materials, which is tied to the *parent part* or finished product (see Figure 5.2). The order of manufacture or assembly is known as the *product hierarchy*. It starts at level 0 for the parent part and continues at levels 1, 2 and so on for the intermediate levels of production. Figure 5.3 shows the product hierarchy for Product 3902. Level 0 is the finished 100-tablet bottle, Level 1 shows the materials required at the packaging stage, and Level 2 shows the raw materials required at the manufacturing stage.

The bill of materials usually incorporates a provision for the expected materials losses that will occur as a normal part of the manufacturing process. Companies use different terms for this provision, such as the *yield factor*, the *scrap factor*, or the *material usage factor*. There is often confusion between the yield factor and the scrap or material usage factor. Both represent losses that occur in the manufacturing processes. However, the

Figure 5.2 Sample Bill of Materials for Product 3902-01

Product Number: **3902-01**

Description: **Multi-A Tablets**

Yield:* **2,360.000**

Item Number	Description	Unit of Measure	Quantity per Batch
M07856	Key Ingredient A	kg	600.0
S09234	Ingredient B	kg	10.8
999231	Ingredient C	kg	800.0
S45321	Ingredient D	kg	27.2

* Yield is expressed per 1,000 tablets, as is common in this industry.

Figure 5.3 Product Hierarchy

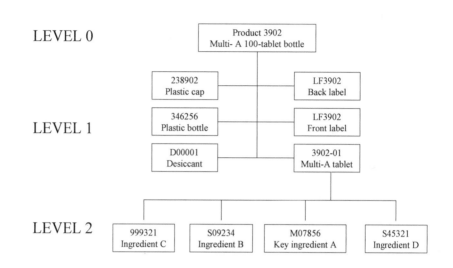

yield factor represents the expected loss under efficient or normal operating conditions and is expressed as a percent of the material input into the process. For example, if the yield factor is 2 percent, 98 percent of the material input into the process will be converted into good output. The 2 percent shortfall may be the result of evaporation losses, residual materials that remain in the production equipment, chemical reactions, or some other reason. From a cost standpoint, the yield factor not only affects materials cost, but also any conversion costs that have been applied up to that stage of the process. The yield factor is commonly used in process industries such as chemicals, pharmaceuticals, and food processing, which make like products in lots or batches in a continuous manner.

The scrap factor is used to adjust the bill of materials (and the related materials cost) for components that are damaged or spoiled in the process. Discrete manufacturers, which make different products as single identifiable items such as printed circuit boards or automobiles, will generally apply a scrap factor at each stage of the manufacturing process. Process manufacturers will typically apply the scrap factor at the packaging stage. The scrap factor is usually expressed as a percent of the materials quantity. Assume that we are packaging 10,000 bottles of tablets (good output) and the bottles have a scrap factor of 2 percent. We will need input of 10,204 bottles from inventory [10,0000 ÷ (1.00 − 0.02) = 10,000 ÷ 0.98], because we expect 204 bottles to be damaged during the packaging process. Figure 5.1 shows how the scrap factor is included in the bill of materials. In this example, the quantity required for the plastic bottle has been rounded 1.02, which includes the 2 percent scrap factor.

Most manufacturing systems allow you to enter a scrap factor in the bill of materials to account for components that are damaged in the process. However, not all systems provide for a yield factor, particularly smaller client/server type applications. In this situation, you will have to develop a workaround to the limitations of your system. You should know and understand how your system handles yield and scrap allowances and the related accounting entries associated with these transactions. Both the yield and scrap factor represent an opportunity for cost improvement.

Materials quantity standards are initially set by the department responsible for product development using one or more of the three methods described below:[1]

1. *Engineering studies* focus on identifying which materials will provide the best combination of quantity, production methods, quality, functionality, and cost. It starts with the preparation of detailed specifications such as engineering drawings, a list of components, or process formulations and uses several techniques such as *value engineering (VE), design for manufacturing and assembly (DFMA)*, and *quality function deployment (QFD)* to determine the optimal use of materials. VE seeks to maximize customer value by increasing functionality and quality while simultaneously reducing costs. DFMA, by contrast, focuses on making the product easier to manufacture while holding functionality levels at a predetermined level. QFD ensures that the customer requirements are not compromised during the design process.

2. *Analysis of past experience* focuses on historical performance. In contrast to the use of engineering studies, this method does not focus on finding the best material available that meets manufacturing criteria. It considers past experience for the same or similar products and uses this data to set materials quantity standards. Because these standards are based on historical performance, they may

include waste and excess usage, which is difficult to determine and isolate. This limitation may be minimized by a reduction in the quantity of material allowed based on expert judgment or industry information. While this method of setting materials standards is less systematic than the use of engineering studies, it is less costly and may be quite satisfactory depending on the business needs of the organization.

3. *Test runs under controlled conditions* avoids one of the principal drawbacks of the past experience method—the incorporation of process inefficiencies in the materials quantity standard. This method determines the standards by performing tests under uniform conditions that can be controlled and replicated. External causes of variations are isolated and eliminated during the test runs. The result is a standard that reflects the expected materials consumption as demonstrated during the test runs.

In smaller organizations that do not have a product development function, an individual familiar with product design and manufacturing operations might set materials quantity standards using the techniques described above.

Accurate materials quantity standards, as described in the BOM, are critical to controlling the conversion process and obtaining reliable cost information. Inaccurate BOMs can result in inaccurate inventory balances, rework, and inefficiencies on the production floor. Once the product is released to manufacturing, engineering or production personnel are typically responsible for maintaining the BOMs. This information should be reviewed at least once a year or whenever there is a significant change in the business. Changes are usually communicated through a formal request called an *Engineering Change Order (ECO)*, which must be authorized by specific individuals in the organization.

Calculating Materials Costs

Materials costs are estimated by multiplying the quantities required in the bill of materials by the cost of each component. There are several types of costs that can be used: average actual cost, standard costs, last costs, and forecast costs. The cost team should determine which type of cost is more appropriate given the purpose of the costing exercise. Types of costs will be discussed in more detail in Chapter 6. The costs of a particular ingredient or component can generally be found in the *item master* of the inventory management system. The item master contains all pertinent information about raw materials, intermediate products, and finished goods, including the unit cost.

A *costed bill of materials* shows the quantity required of each component, its unit cost, and the extended total cost of each component based on the usage required. It then adds all the component costs to obtain a total cost per unit or per batch. Figure 5.4 shows the costed bill of materials for Product 3902, one 100-tablet bottle of Multi-A vitamins. In this example, the unit of measure is one bottle and the costed bill of materials is the sum of the materials costs of each ingredient or component that makes up the product. The lower level item, 3902-01, is costed in a slightly different manner because it is produced in batches of 2,360,000 tablets, which is the expected manufacturing yield. In this situation, the unit cost is the average cost per tablet, which is calculated by dividing the total materials cost of the production batch by the manufacturing yield. Figure 5.5 shows the unit cost calculation for Product 3902-01. Note that the unit of measure for yield and costing purposes is expressed per 1,000 tablets, a measure commonly used in the pharmaceutical industry. The costing issues surrounding yield will be discussed in more detail in Chapter 6.

Figure 5.6 summarizes our discussion on calculating materials cost. It shows how to perform the calculation, which individuals in the organization are responsible for providing and updating information, and a list of factors that could affect the quantity required or the cost of a component. The quantity required for manufacturing or assembling a product is a function of the product or process design. Therefore, any major change in the product design, the production process, or the manufacturing technology should prompt a review of the bill of materials. As stated before, engineering or manufacturing operations typically have responsibility for keeping the bill of materials current. Accountants usually do not have the technical know-how to perform this task.

The estimated cost of a component should be provided by the purchasing function and consider a number of factors that may affect costs

Figure 5.4 Costed Bill of Materials for Product 3902

Product Number: **3902**
Description: **Multi-A 100-tablet bottle**

Item Number	Description	Unit of Measure	Quantity per Bottle	Unit Cost (in USD)	Total Cost (in USD)
3902-01	Multi-A tablets	per thousand	0.10	$14.086	$ 1.409
346256	White plastic bottle	ea	1.02	$ 0.030	$ 0.031
238902	Cap plastic metal	ea	1.02	$ 0.010	$ 0.010
LF3902	Front label	ea	1.05	$ 0.005	$ 0.005
LB3902	Back label	ea	1.05	$ 0.005	$ 0.005
D00001	Dessicant	ea	1.04	$ 0.020	$ 0.021
CX1236	Circular	ea	1.04	$ 0.020	$ 0.021
Total materials cost					**$ 1.502**

Figure 5.5 Costed Bill of Materials for Product 3902-01

Product Number: **3902-01**
Description: **Multi-A Tablets**
Yield:* **2,360.000**

Item Number	Description	Unit of Measure	Quantity per Bottle	Unit Cost (in USD)	Total Cost (in USD)
M07856	Key Ingredient A	kg	600	$50.00	$30,000
S09234	Ingredient B	kg	10.8	$28.00	$ 302
999231	Ingredient C	kg	800	$ 1.85	$ 1,480
S45321	Ingredient D	kg	27.2	$11.15	$ 303
Total materials cost per batch					**$32,085**
Cost per 1,000 tablets					**$13.595**

(total materials cost ÷ yield = $32,085 ÷ 2,360.00 = $13.595)

* Yield is expressed per 1,000 tablets, as is common in this industry.

Figure 5.6 How to Calculate Materials Costs

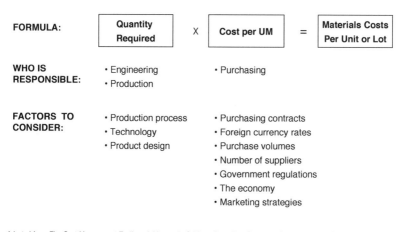

| FORMULA: | Quantity Required | X | Cost per UM | = | Materials Costs Per Unit or Lot |

WHO IS RESPONSIBLE:
- Engineering
- Production
- Purchasing

FACTORS TO CONSIDER:
- Production process
- Technology
- Product design

- Purchasing contracts
- Foreign currency rates
- Purchase volumes
- Number of suppliers
- Government regulations
- The economy
- Marketing strategies

such as freight, purchasing discounts, number of suppliers, economic trends, and government regulations. Government regulations can affect material costs if they have a local sourcing requirement or assess duties on imported parts. Therefore, estimating the component costs is more complex than simply analyzing historical trends. Purchasing should consider future trends or requirements, as well as past performance, in estimating materials costs.

LABOR COSTS

Direct labor costs are the total compensation costs of employees who work directly on manufacturing the product or providing the service to the customer. Total compensation includes wages, salaries, payroll taxes, fringe benefits, and overtime. *Indirect labor costs* are the total compensation costs of those employees that support the manufacturing or service process. Indirect labor employees may include mechanics, data entry clerks, supervisors, warehouse employees, and others. Indirect labor costs are generally included in overhead costs.

Labor standards are traditionally used to estimate labor costs, particularly in a manufacturing setting or repetitive service operations. *Labor standards* are the estimated time an employee should take to complete an operation. Labor standards are based on engineering studies, historical data, or management estimates. We will discuss how to set time standards in more detail in Chapter 6.

Manufacturing organizations typically set standards for labor-intensive operations such as apparel manufacturing, assembly operations, and packaging and compare these to the actual labor hours used. This information is used to measure performance, control the manufacturing operations, and look for cost improvement opportunities. Due to the increased automation of manufacturing and service processes, many companies have eliminated the use of labor standards and detailed labor tracking for control purposes. In many organizations, particularly in the service sector, labor standards are used primarily for headcount planning and profitability analysis.

Labor standards are usually found in the *routing* file or some similar software application that contains the sequence of operations that will be performed on the product and the detailed labor hours, machine hours, and the *setup time* that will be required by each operation.[2] Some software applications combine the routing file and the bill of materials into one application that serves both purposes. If your company uses labor standards, the costing process is fairly simple. The labor costs are calculated by multiplying the standard labor hours required for each operation by an average wage rate. The average wage rate should include the base salary, the payroll taxes, and the fringe benefits. Let us return to our example of Multi-A. Since the manufacturing process is highly automated, labor hours are calculated by multiplying the expected process times by the number of employees required in each operation. The routing file for this product and the labor cost calculation are shown in Figure 5.7. In this example, labor is a relatively insignificant cost component relative to materials. Therefore, one decision that could be made by the product team is whether to report direct labor as a separate cost component or include it as part of overhead costs.[3]

Figure 5.8 shows the formula for calculating labor costs and a list of those factors that could affect the labor standards or the average wage rates. It also shows the parties responsible for providing and updating the labor standards and cost information. Similar to materials quantity standards, labor standards are initially set at the product development stage

Figure 5.7 How to Calculate Total Labor Costs

Operation	PROCESS HOURS		LABOR HOURS*			
	Production	Setup	Number of Employees	Production Labor	Setup Labor	Total
Weighing	1.0	0.5	2.0	2.0	1.0	3.0
Blending	4.0	1.0	4.0	16.0	4.0	20.0
Compression	8.0	1.0	1.0	8.0	1.0	9.0
Total hours per lot	13.0	2.5		26.0	6.0	32.0
Average wage rate (given)				$12.00	$12.00	$12.00

Total labor costs per lot**		$312.00	$72.00	$384.00
Labor cost per thousand tablets***		$0.132	$0.031	$0.163

* Labor hours = Production or setup hours x number of employees
** Labor costs per lot = Production or setup labor hours x average wage rate
*** Labor costs per lot ÷ standard yield (2,360.0 thousand tablets; see Figure 5.5)

and later updated as the product is released to manufacturing by production or engineering personnel. The techniques of VE, DFMA, and QFD also apply to the use of labor standards.

An alternative method of assigning labor costs to products or services is on a per-unit basis. For example, suppose you operate a service call center that has 40 employees and provides service 24 hours per day, 7 days per week. One way to assign labor costs would be on a per call basis, dividing the total labor costs of the customer service representatives by the number of calls handled during the period. Though this calculation is straightforward and simple, it assumes that all calls consume the same amount of labor resources per call. However, if the call center provides diverse services (payment processing, customer complaints, account inquiry) that require different labor times, this costing assumption would not be appropriate. In this situation, costs should be developed based on labor standards or estimates, defined in terms of average minutes per type

Figure 5.8 How to Calculate Labor Costs

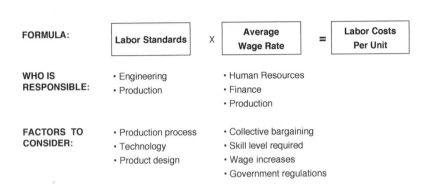

of call, and then multiplying these estimates by the average labor costs per minute.

In service organizations, labor will usually represent a larger portion of total costs than materials or supplies and should be a primary focus of the project team. How labor costs are calculated will have a significant impact on the overall accuracy of the cost information prepared by the organization.

OVERHEAD COSTS

Overhead costs are indirect costs that cannot be directly traced to a product or service in a cost-effective manner. They include expenses such as minor tools or equipment, supplies, training, depreciation, and utilities, among others. They also may include charges allocated from departments that provide support services such as purchasing, warehouse, engineering, and information systems.

Overhead costs are typically collected by departments or work areas. Because they cannot be traced specifically to the product, service, or customer, they must be assigned to these items in a reasonable manner to obtain the full cost of the item being measured.[4] The *cost assignment* or *allocation base* is a factor that links the indirect costs to the item being measured.

Although there are several different criteria than can be used to choose the proper assignment base, I favor the cause-effect criterion because it ties the allocation of the indirect costs more directly to the business processes. In manufacturing organizations, some common examples of allocation bases are labor hours, machine hours, cycle time, and units. In service organizations indirect costs are typically assigned using labor hours or on a per unit basis (i.e., per call, per customer, per patient, per passenger-mile, among others). Figure 5.9 shows how the overhead allocation process works.

Let us apply the previous discussion on overhead costs calculation to our Multi-A example. Because the manufacturing process is highly automated, its accountants have determined that process hours are the most appropriate basis to assign overhead costs. Assume that the total overhead costs for the production department that manufactures Multi-A is $1,000,000 per year. Total process hours for all products manufactured in this department, including setup time, are 20,000 hours based on forecasted production volumes. The overhead rate for this area would be $50

Figure 5.9 The Overhead Allocation Process

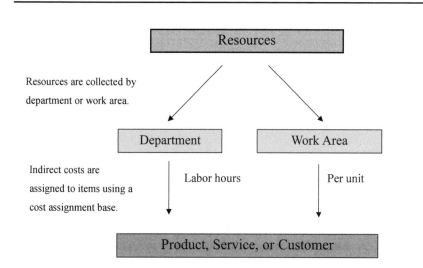

per process hour ($1,000,000 ÷ 20,000 hours). Therefore, the overhead costs assigned to Multi-A would equal $775 per lot ($50 per hour x 15.5 process hours) or $0.328 per thousand tablets [$775 ÷ 2,360,000 tablets]. The overhead cost calculations for Multi-A are summarized in Figure 5.10.

Most companies have different overhead rates for each department or work area. Only those products or services that flow through the area are charged with the overhead costs for that area. If a cost that has traditionally been included in overhead is significant and can be specifically identified to a product or service, it should not be included as an overhead cost. For example, most costing systems include depreciation as part of the overhead rate. At one of my clients, however, we identified a $1,000,000 production line that was 100 percent dedicated to a particular product. Under the old costing system, the depreciation costs associated with this equipment were allocated to all products through the overhead rate. Under the new system, these depreciation costs were charged directly to the specific product that was manufactured on this line, providing a more accurate representation of its true production costs.

Figure 5.10 How to Assign Overhead Costs

Operation	PROCESS HOURS		
	Production	Setup	Total
Weighing	1.0	0.5	1.5
Blending	4.0	1.0	5.0
Compression	8.0	1.0	9.0
Total hours per lot	13.0	2.5	15.5
Overhead rate (given)	$50.00	$50.00	$50.00
Overhead costs per lot*	$650.00	$125.00	$775.00
Overhead costs per unit**	$0.275	$0.053	$0.328

* Overhead costs = Production or setup process hours x overhead rate
** Overhead costs per lot ÷ standard yield (2,360.0 thousand tablets; see Figure 5.5)

COST ROLLUP

Once we have calculated the individual cost elements of the item being measured, we are ready to perform a cost rollup. The *cost rollup* is an accounting process that adds up the significant cost components and calculates the total or unit cost as required. Generally, these cost components are broken down into labor, materials, and overhead; in some service organizations, materials will be an insignificant cost and will not be reported separately. In manufacturing, costs are rolled up according to the product hierarchy. Therefore, the intermediate product or subassembly costs are calculated first and this number is used to determine the cost of the finished product. Figure 5.11 shows the cost rollup for Product 3902-01. Note that the costs of Product 3902-01, $14.086 per 1,000 tablets, are rolled up as part of the materials costs into Product 3902, one 100-tablet bottle of Multi-A (see Figure 5.4). Labor and overhead costs from a prior level can be rolled up into the materials costs of the next level or maintain their separate identities throughout the various levels of the product hierarchy. The decision to maintain these costs separate will depend on management's information needs and the capabilities of your information systems application.

In service organizations, a cost rollup is necessary when the transaction or service being costed goes through several stages. Figure 5.12 shows the different activities associated with processing a check at a financial institution. At each stage of the process, a unit cost is calculated for this particular type of transaction. The cost rollup would sum the unit cost of each activity to determine the total unit cost of this type of transaction. The costs of branch activities are highlighted because it is the sum of the various activities that occur at the branch level starting at the teller station and ending with the packet that is prepared and sent to the bank operations center. It is equivalent to an intermediate product or subassembly in manufacturing, which must be rolled up to obtain the total costs of this transaction. Note that a detailed cost breakdown is not done by individual cost component (labor, materials, and overhead), but by activity or process.

Once the cost rollup is completed, the unit costs should be compared against a budgeted, expected, or actual cost for reasonableness. If these costs are unavailable (such as when an item is being costed for the first time), industry benchmarks or cost of similar items can be used to validate the calculated costs. Line managers should review and approve all costs. If a

Figure 5.11 Cost Roll-Up Example for Multi-A Tablet:Product 3902-01

Product Number: **3902-01**

Description: **Multi-A Tablets**

Yield: **2,360.000**

MATERIALS

Item Number	Description	UM	Quantity per Bottle	Unit Cost (in USD)	Total Cost (in USD)	Unit Cost per 1,000 tablets
M07856	Key Ingredient A	kg	600	$50.00	$30,000	$12.712
S09234	Ingredient B	kg	10.8	$28.00	302	0.128
999231	Ingredient C	kg	800	$ 1.85	1,480	0.627
S45321	Ingredient D	kg	27.2	$ 11.15	303	0.128
Subtotal materials cost per batch					**$32,085**	**$13.595**

LABOR

	Weighing	hr	3.0	$ 12.00	$ 36	$ 0.015
	Granulation	hr	20.0	$ 12.00	240	0.102
	Compression	hr	9.0	$ 12.00	108	0.046
Subtotal labor cost per batch					**$ 384**	**$ 0.163**

OVERHEAD

	Weighing	hr	1.5	$50.00	$ 75	$ 0.032
	Granulation	hr	5.0	$50.00	250	0.106
	Compression	hr	9.0	$50.00	450	0.190
Subtotal overhead cost per batch					**$ 775**	**$ 0.328**

| **Total costs*** | | | | | **$33,244** | **$14.086** |

* Total costs = materials cost + labor cost + overhead cost

  Total costs per batch =$32,085 + $384 + $775 = $33,244; Unit costs = $33,244 ÷ 2,360 = $14.086

Figure 5.12 Cost Roll-Up of Check Cashing Service

Service: **Check Cashing**

Activity	Unit Cost (in USD)
Perform branch activities	$1.00
Receive checks	0.01
Input and code checks	0.03
Microfilm and sort transactions	0.02
Balance and correct transactions	0.15
Process transactions in system	0.07
Total cost per check	**$1.28**

cost seems out of line with prior experience, or if in the judgment of the line manager, a cost is too high or too low, the cost analysts should reexamine the assumptions that underlie the cost calculations such as time standards, yield, scrap, and allowances in conjunction with operations personnel. The line managers should agree that the costing methodology and the operational parameters upon which the cost calculations are based provide a fair representation of the resources consumed to manufacture a product, provide a service, or manage a customer.

SUMMARY

This chapter has provided a general overview of how to calculate the cost of a product or service. Although in theory the mechanics are fairly straight-forward, in practice, the cost calculation methodology can become quite intricate due to the complexities of the business processes. Each company, even within the same industry, will have its own peculiarities, which must be handled within the cost model. The objective of the project team should be to develop a cost model that provides a reasonably accurate representation of the resources required to manufacture a product or provide a service in the simplest manner possible.

The development of the cost model will require agreement on the operational parameters that underlie the cost calculation and will raise key issues that must be decided by the team. We have touched on some issues in this chapter. Chapter 6 will present a more detailed discussion on some of the more difficult issues that will be encountered by the team and what the implications are for the costs of their organization.

ENDNOTES

1. For more information, see *Standard Costs and Variance Analysis* (Montvale, N.J.: Institute of Management Accountants, 1974), 26–51.

2. *Setup time* is the preparation time involved in the production or service delivery process. It may involve equipment installation, documentation, entering run parameters, clean-up and other miscellaneous activities at the start and the end of a process. In manufacturing, setup time usually has two components: labor, which is the time the employee spends setting up the equipment, and machine time, which is the time the machine is nonoperational. For example, if it takes two employees 30 minutes to set up and clean the equipment, the setup time would consist of one hour of labor (2 employees x 30 minutes) and 30 minutes of machine time. Examples of setup time include time spent on the installation and removal of equipment, cleaning time, the time spent entering the machine parameters, or the time running the machine before the first good output is produced.

3. The sum of direct labor and overhead costs is known as *conversion costs*.

4. For an ample discussion on the two-stage allocation procedure that forms the basis of most modern cost systems, see Robin Cooper, "The Two-Stage Procedure in Cost Accounting: Part One," *Journal of Cost Management* (Summer 1987): 43–51; and "The Two-Stage Procedure in Cost Accounting: Part Two," *Journal of Cost Management* (Fall 1987): 39–45.

6

Costing Issues

During the development of the costing system, the team will have to address certain issues that affect not only how costs are developed, but also how they are collected and reported down the road. There are no right or wrong answers, and the approaches taken by the team will depend on the state of organizational development, the system applications, and the organizational philosophy toward cost management. Advanced organizations with highly developed information systems may take a different approach than a start-up operation that has a limited infrastructure to manage costs. Moreover, organizations that form part of larger corporate structure may have to conform to standardized policies and practices, which may or may not adequately address these issues.

In this chapter, we will present the significant issues that should be discussed and agreed on during the design and development of the costing model and subsequent systems setup and test. These issues will be presented from an operational and financial perspective. They relate to capacity utilization, yield or process efficiency, labor productivity, data collection and analysis, cost types, and costing methods. The discussion and resolution of these issues will provide a critical link between the business processes and reported costs allowing managers to grasp how their decisions affect the cost structure of the organization. Moreover, they allow managers to identify cost improvement opportunities from both a strategic and operational standpoint.

CAPACITY UTILIZATION

Capacity is an elusive concept. At a macro level, it can be defined as the value-creating ability of the resources available to the organization or the ability of the business to meet market demand. At a micro level it can have several definitions: (a) the value-creating potential of a process, (b) the amount of output that can be obtained from a process, (c) an upper limit or constraint on the work that an operating unit can handle, or (d) an estimate of the work done by a fixed set of resources.[1] In practice, capacity is typically defined as the output that can be achieved over a particular time period. Output is expressed in units, labor hours, process hours, or some other reasonable measure, while time is measured in years, months, days, hours, minutes, or seconds. From a costing standpoint, the team needs to understand the definition of capacity for their organization, what factors affect capacity, and how it will be linked to the costs of the resources available.

There are several baseline measures of capacity. The *maximum or theoretical capacity* represents the maximum amount of work that a process or facility can produce operating 24 hours per day, 7 days per week with zero waste. No adjustments are made for the nonproductive uses of available resources including holidays, weekends, planned downtime, or any other possible constraints on the manufacturing or service delivery process. Theoretical capacity assumes that the firm operates at its maximum potential all the time. Therefore, if we assume 365 days per year, the maximum capacity for any particular process would 8,760 hours per year [24 hours per day X 365 days per year]. *Practical* or *design capacity* can be defined as the level of output that can be obtained from a particular operation, given the current process specifications and the system design. It takes into consideration holidays, planned downtime, and any other unavoidable factors that may limit the availability of resources for productive purposes. The *available capacity* is the maximum output that can be produced given a fixed level of resources. It is typically based on the number of manned shifts. For example, if you are only staffed to run one shift instead of three, your available capacity would be the maximum output that you could produce in one shift, given this level of resources. The *planned* or *scheduled capacity* is the amount of output that is projected for a particular time period. The planned capacity can be above, below, or at available capacity. It is usually the basis for the annual business plan, financial forecasts, and standard costs.

Although these definitions of capacity may seem fairly clear-cut, in practice capacity measurement can be quite difficult. Suppose you have a service process that is designed to handle several types of transactions. The maximum service capacity of this operation is 24 hours a day.

However, if each type of transaction has a different processing time, the maximum output that can be obtained from this process will vary, depending on the number and type of transactions that are received on any given day. What output would you assign as the maximum capacity for this operation? The answer to this question is not easy and illustrates some of the subtleties of capacity measurement. Unless you have a dedicated production or service line, the capacity of a particular process may vary according to the types of products or services that run through this line. If you define capacity in terms of output, you will have to make some inherent assumptions about the mix of products or services that you can provide in a given time period. Line managers should understand and agree on the assumptions that underlie these capacity calculations.

The Consortium for Advanced Manufacturing-International (CAM-I) has proposed an alternate framework for analyzing capacity, which focuses on time as the basis for capacity measurement.[2] Time provides a simple mechanism to link capacity utilization and cost. It is within this framework that we will discuss the issues surrounding capacity measurement and its impact on product or service cost. Appendix B describes time-based capacity models in more detail and how these can be coupled with cost information to provide better information for decision-making purposes.

When time or the level of output is used as the basis for capacity measurement, we run up against another challenge: the bottleneck or constraining factor. A process is composed of activities or operations that have inputs and outputs. The output of one operation will be the input into the next. Usually, there is one activity or operation that limits the entire process. *Theory of constraints (TOC)* maintains that any system has at least one constraint that limits throughput and the ability to generate profits.[3] TOC focuses on identifying the system constraint, letting the constraint set the pace of the system, and focusing improvement efforts on liberating the constraint. When one constraint is lifted, usually another factor will become the constraint and the process starts over again. TOC advocates maintain that liberating capacity in nonconstrained operations will not improve the bottom line because the capacity of the entire process is dictated by the constraining operation.[4]

The TOC methodology involves identifying the system constraint, deciding how to optimize its use, and subordinating all other elements of the system to the constraining factor. Suppose you own a wholesale bakery that supplies major supermarkets with ready-to-eat baked goods. The production process involves several operations, as shown in Figure 6.1: weighing the ingredients, mixing them, preparing the mix for baking, baking, cooling, finishing the product, and packaging for shipment. Your line managers have identified the number of ovens in the baking operation to be the system constraint. Applying a TOC methodology, you would ensure that the ovens are 100 percent utilized and that the capacity of all other operations is aligned to the capacity of the ovens. In this manner, you do not burden the system with excess capacity in operations that will not increase throughput.

One key decision that the project team must make is how it will measure practical and available capacity—whether in terms of total available hours or based on the availability of the constraining operation. If a TOC approach is used, the capacity of the entire process will be subordinate to the capacity of the constraining operation. Other operations should be run so as to keep the constraining operation running at its most efficient level, as defined by line management. Gray and Leonard summarized the challenges of capacity measurement as follows:

Figure 6.1 Production Process for Ready-to-Eat Products

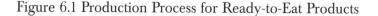

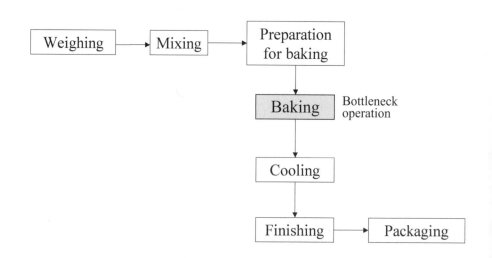

Capacity depends upon what you assume to be fixed (i.e., the number of shifts, or the number of available workers), and the time frame of the decision being analyzed. Changing these factors may even change the resource that is the bottleneck. The measure of capacity that is the most useful depends upon the type of decision being made. Capacity over the current number of shifts being worked is probably appropriate when evaluating the impact of an investment in a new preventative maintenance program. . . . Evaluating when it will be necessary to purchase new equipment, however, requires a different set of assumptions. . . . Think carefully about the operating environment and the decision at hand before you begin a capacity analysis.[5]

Cost calculations usually are based on an assumption of capacity utilization. *Capacity utilization* is the extent to which a firm uses its productive capacity. It can significantly affect unit cost and the perceived profitability of a product. When a company establishes a manufacturing or service operation, it has recurring costs that are independent of volume such as rent, depreciation, and facility maintenance costs. In addition, it may wish to maintain a fixed level of employees to manage the monthly fluctuations in customer demand. When an operation works at the desired capacity level, it is making maximum utilization of these resources. However, if it operates below this capacity, traditional costing practices will charge the cost of this excess capacity to its current products or services. A simplified real-world example will illustrate this point.

Suppose Company XYZ has a highly automated manufacturing operation that can work three shifts per day, 360 days per year. Its theoretical capacity would be 8,640 hours per year.[6] However, of the total 360 workdays available, the plant is only scheduled to work 260 days during the year. Therefore, its practical capacity is 6,240 hours per year.[7] Due to limitations in market demand, it is currently running only two eight-hour shifts, five days a week, 48 weeks per year. Consequently, its available capacity is 4,160 hours.[8]

In this operation, Company XYZ manufactures Product X. This product requires five hours of process time and has a budgeted volume of 60,000 units per year. Its budgeted capacity is 3,000 hours, which is calculated by multiplying the budgeted volume by the standard process hours per unit.[9] How do these different capacity scenarios affect the product costs? Let us assume that the budgeted overhead costs of this manufacturing operation are one million dollars ($1,000,000) and that these costs are assigned to products based on standard process hours. Figure 6.2 shows the overhead costs per standard process hour under each capacity scenario described here. The cost per process hour can range from a low of $116 using the theoretical hours of 8,640 as the cost assignment basis to a high of $333 using standard process hours based on budgeted volumes.

Figure 6.2 Overhead Costs per Process Hour under Different Capacity Scenarios

Number of annual workdays	360
Number of scheduled workdays	260
Number of eight-hour shifts	3
Manned shifts per day	2
Budgeted volume (units)	60,000
Standard process hours per unit	0.05
Total overhead costs	$ 1,000,000

Description	Theoretical Capacity	Practical Capacity	Available Capacity	Budgeted Capacity
Total overhead costs	$1,000,000	$1,000,000	$1,000,000	$1,000,000
Process hours available (1)	8,640	6,240	4,160	3,000
Cost per process hour (2)	$116	$160	$240	$333

(1) Process hours available = number of workdays x number of shifts x 8 hours per shift
   Theoretical capacity = 360 days x 3 shifts x 8 hours = 8,640 hours
   Practical capacity = 260 days x 3 shifts x 8 hours = 6,240 hours
   Available capacity = 260 days x 2 shifts x 8 hours = 4,160 hours
   Budgeted capacity = 60,000 units x 0.05 per unit = 3,000 hours

(2) Cost per process hour = total overhead costs ÷ process hours available as calculated in (1) above.

Figure 6.3 shows the impact of capacity utilization on product cost. Assuming the fixed and variable cost structure remains constant over all four capacity scenarios, the use of budgeted capacity would result in a unit cost that is $10.85 higher than theoretical capacity, $8.65 higher than practical capacity, and $4.65 higher than available capacity. The difference between the unit cost using budgeted capacity and the unit cost using theoretical, practical, or available capacity represents the cost of excess capacity that is being charged to Product X. For example, the use of budgeted versus available capacity would result in an additional $5 per unit, or $280,000 of overhead costs being charged to Product X. These costs bear no relationship to the fundamental economics of the production process and add no value to the product or the end customer.

In this simple example, we assumed that the fixed and variable cost structure remained unchanged in all four scenarios. However, it is important to differentiate between managed and committed capacity costs when measuring the costs of capacity.[10] *Committed capacity costs* are those that are unavoidable in the short to intermediate term and include items such as building rent, depreciation, security, insurance, and non-refundable service contracts. These costs are considered fixed and do not fluctuate with changes in capacity utilization. *Managed capacity costs* are those that are avoidable in the short to intermediate term and typically include labor, utilities, and supplies among others. These costs will increase or decrease with changes in the utilization levels, though not necessarily on a proportional basis. The classification of managed and committed costs will be unique to each organization. For example, a facility with a no-layoff policy may consider direct labor a committed cost, while another similar facility might classify it as a managed cost. Let us return to the prior example of Company XYZ to see how the identification of committed and managed costs might affect the cost calculations.

Suppose the $1,000,000 of estimated overhead costs are based on available capacity, which consists of two eight-hour shifts, 260 days per year. If demand were to suddenly increase to practical capacity levels, it is unrealistic to assume that these costs will remain unchanged. At a minimum, you would expect that the increased volume levels would generate a corresponding increase in certain types of costs such as indirect labor, electricity, water, maintenance, and supplies. It is unrealistic to calculate a

Figure 6.3 Cost of Excess Capacity under Different Capacity Scenarios

Number of annual workdays	360
Number of scheduled workdays	260
Number of eight-hour shifts	3
Manned shifts per day	2
Budgeted volume (units)	60,000
Standard process hours per unit	0.05
Total overhead costs	$ 1,000,000

Description	Theoretical Capacity	Practical Capacity	Available Capacity	Budgeted Capacity*
Total overhead costs	$1,000,000	$1,000,000	$1,000,000	$1,000,000
Process hours available (1)	8,640	6,240	4,160	3,000
Cost per process hour (2)	$116	$160	$240	$333
Standard process hours per unit	0.05	0.05	0.05	0.05
Cost per unit (3)	$5.80	$8.00	$12.00	$16.65
Total overhead costs charged to Product X (4)	$348,000	$480,000	$720,000	$999,000
Cost of excess capacity (5)	$652,000	$520,000	$280,000	–

(1) See Figure 6.2
(2) See Figure 6.2
(3) Cost per unit = cost per process hour x standard process hours per unit
(4) Total costs charged to product = cost per unit x budgeted volume
(5) Cost of excess capacity = total overhead costs less total overhead costs charged to products

* The total overhead costs charged to Product X in this scenario have a rounding difference of $1,000 that is not significant.

cost per hour based on practical capacity, which assumes that the managed capacity costs will remain unchanged at these volume levels. If the production levels at Company XYZ rose to 8,400 hours per year, we would expect the managed capacity costs to increase accordingly, although not necessarily in proportion to the increase in volume.

An alternative scenario to calculate the cost of excess capacity would be to calculate two separate overhead rates: one for committed costs based on practical capacity and another for managed costs based on available capacity. This alternative is called the *mixed scenario*. Committed costs are generally considered fixed and will not change with increases or decreases in volume. A company could produce at or below the practical capacity level and experience no change in these types of costs. Conversely, managed costs are *variable, semivariable* or *step-fixed costs*, and will increase or decrease with changes in volume or product mix.[11] Suppose the $1,000,000 budgeted costs of Company XYZ consisted of $250,000 of committed costs and $750,000 of managed costs. How would the excess cost calculation change under this mixed scenario? Figure 6.4 shows the cost of excess capacity based on four capacity scenarios—practical, mixed, available, and budgeted—and separates committed from managed costs in the calculation of the overhead rate. Theoretical capacity is not included because, in practice, managers would be unwilling to accept costs calculated under ideal operating conditions, particularly if used to evaluate organizational performance. Note that the cost of excess capacity for committed costs is the same in the practical and mixed capacity scenario. However, the cost of excess capacity for managed costs under the mixed scenario is significantly lower than the practical capacity scenario. The use of a mixed scenario assumes that in order to reach practical capacity levels the organization will incur incremental costs not currently contemplated in the budget.

The treatment of unused capacity costs is an important design issue that should be explicitly addressed by the project team. Traditionally, accountants have calculated products and service costs based on *full cost absorption*. This methodology requires that all costs incurred to manufacture a product or provide a service be "absorbed" or included in the unit cost calculation. This practice, which still permeates most cost systems, allows companies to hide the cost of excess capacity in the overhead cost of their products. It has several dysfunctional consequences for the organization. First, it distorts the profitability of products or services because it charges these items for resources they did not consume. This situation may cause profitable items to appear as unprofitable or uncompetitive in the marketplace. Second, it may lead to poor management decisions. Management may decide to remove products or services from its sales offerings based

Figure 6.4 Cost of Excess Capacity under Different Capacity Scenarios Separating Committed and Managed Costs

Number of annual workdays	360
Number of scheduled workdays	260
Number of eight-hour shifts	3
Manned shifts per day	2
Budgeted volume (units)	60,000
Standard process hours per unit	0.05
Total overhead costs	$ 1,000,000

Description	Practical Capacity	Mixed Capacity	Available Capacity	Budgeted Capacity*
Overhead costs				
• Commited costs	$250,000	$250,000	$250,000	$250,000
• Managed costs	750,000	750,000	750,000	750,000
Total overhead costs	**$1,000,000**	**$1,000,000**	**$1,000,000**	**$1,000,000**
Process hours available (1)				
• Commited capacity	6,240	6,240	4,160	3,000
• Managed capacity	6,240	4,160	4,160	3,000
Standard hours per unit	**0.05**	**0.05**	**0.05**	**0.05**
Cost per hour (2)				
• Commited costs	$40	$40	$60	$83
• Managed costs	120	180	180	250
Total costs per hour	**$160**	**$220**	**$240**	**$333**
Cost per unit (3)				
• Commited costs	$2.0	$2.0	$3.0	$4.15
• Managed costs	6.0	9.0	9.0	12.50
Total costs per unit	**$8.0**	**$11.0**	**$12.0**	**$16.67**
Overhead costs charged to products (4)				
• Commited costs	$120,000	$120,000	$180,000	$249,000
• Managed costs	360,000	540,000	540,000	750,000
Total costs per unit	**$480,000**	**$660,000**	**$720,000**	**$999,000**
The cost of excess capacity (5)				
• Commited costs	$130,000	$130,000	$70,000	–
• Managed costs	390,000	210,000	210,000	–
Total costs per unit	**$520,000**	**$340,000**	**$280,000**	**–**

(1) The process hours available are the same under the practical and mixed capacity scenario and equal three 8-hour shifts, 260 days per year. For the available and budgeted scenario, it is the same calculation as in Figure 6.2.

(2) Cost per process hour = total overhead costs ÷ process hours available as calculated in (1).

(3) Cost per unit = cost per process hour × standard process hours per unit

(4) Total costs charged to product = cost per unit × budgeted volume

(5) Cost of excess capacity = total overhead costs less total overhead costs charged to products

* The total overhead costs charged to Product X in this scenario have a rounding difference of $1,000 that is not significant.

on inaccurate cost information, thinking this action will improve the company's bottom line. However, fixed overhead costs do not go away with decreases in production or sales volume, particularly committed capacity costs. As uncompetitive products are dropped, the fixed overhead costs that had been assigned to these products are redistributed among the remaining products or services. As a result, the reported costs of the remaining products increase, and now these products become uncompetitive and are either outsourced or dropped. The cycle repeats itself in a downward spin known in accounting circles as the *death spiral*.[12] Eventually the facility shuts down or the company goes out of business.

In manufacturing circles, accounting practitioners contend that all manufacturing costs should be included in the unit cost and should be reported as cost of sales when the products are sold. Cost management experts disagree with this approach.[13] They claim that excess capacity is an ongoing cost of running the business, which is unrelated to the products manufactured during the period. These costs should not be included in the product cost calculation, but expensed directly into cost of sales as a separate line item on the income statement. They maintain that this accounting treatment has several advantages. First, it provides a more accurate representation of the true economics of production by eliminating the cost of excess capacity from the cost calculations. Second, excess capacity, formerly buried in the product costs, becomes a visible item on the income statement spurring management to take action. Unfortunately, accountants are still reluctant to report excess capacity in this manner. Though some more forward-thinking companies are calculating the cost of excess capacity, they often revert to a full cost absorption model when calculating and reporting their costs.

Service organizations have similar issues with capacity cost management. They too have excess capacity that is buried in their financial statements. Suppose you are a distributor with a 100,000 square feet warehouse, which rents for $400,000 per year. Due to market conditions, only 50 percent of the warehouse is currently being used. The cost of excess capacity for this distributor would be $200,000 ($400,000 x 50%), which represents the unused portion of the warehouse.

Excess capacity issues can not only distort the financial performance of an organization, but also lead to suboptimal pricing decisions, particularly if these are based on costs. Another example will illustrate this point. Data Processing, Inc. is a service bureau that processes accounts payable and payroll transactions for its customers. In the accounts payable area, it has 10 clerks that work an average of 1,750 hours per year. Labor costs, including payroll taxes and benefits, are $18,000 per clerk. On average, each clerk can process around 12,000 invoices per year. Overhead costs are around $150,000 per year. The cost per invoice, based on the available capacity of the firm, is $2.75 (see Figure 6.5). If the company wished to obtain a 20 percent profit margin on its processing services, it would set its price per invoice at $3.44.[14] Now suppose the projected volume level for the current year was 100,000 invoices. The company believes that this is not a permanent drop in the business and decides not to lay off any clerks. The cost per invoice now increases to $3.30 (see Figure 6.6). If the company maintains its current pricing model, it would have to raise its price per invoice to $4.13 in order to recover its costs and maintain its desired profit margin. This increase could price the company right out of the market.

Figure 6.5 Cost per Invoice Based on Available Capacity

Description	Available Capacity
Labor cost per clerk	$ 18,000
Number of clerks	10
Total labor costs per year	$180,000
Overhead costs	$150,000
Total costs	$330,000
Expected output*	120,000
Cost per invoice**	$2.75

* Expected output is based on capacity available, which is defined as the maximum invoices that can be processed with 10 clerks. It is calculated by multiplying the number of clerks by the average number of invoices processed per year (12,000 invoices per clerk per year x 10 clerks)

** Cost per invoice = $330,000 ÷ 120,000 = $2.75

Figure 6.6 Comparison of Cost per Invoice Based on Available
and Scheduled Capacity

Description	Available Capacity	Scheduled Capacity
Labor cost per clerk	$18,000	$18,000
Number of clerks	10	10
Total labor costs per year	$180,000	$180,000
Overhead costs	$150,000	$150,000
Total costs	$330,000	$330,000
Expected output	120,000	100,000
Cost per invoice*	$2.75	$3.30
The cost of excess capacity**		$55,000

* Expected output is based on two capacity scenarios: available capacity, which is defined as the maximum invoices that can be processed with 10 clerks and scheduled capacity, based on projected volumes for the next year. It is calculated by multiplying the number of clerks by the average number of invoices processed per year (12,000 invoices per clerk per year x 10 clerks)

** The cost of excess capacity is calculated as follows:

Total capacity costs	$330,000
Capacity utilized ($2.75 per invoice x 100,000 invoices)	275,000
Excess or unused capacity	$ 55,000

As we have seen from this discussion, capacity cost measurement is an important issue that must be specifically addressed by the project team. This decision should not be left solely to the accountants. Though the team may decide to cost its products or services based on full costs, it should have a mechanism to understand how much, if any, excess capacity is hidden in these costs. Many cost applications provide the capability to enter more than one cost for a product or service. If this is the case, I recommend that the cost system calculate two costs: one based on scheduled capacity and another based on available or practical capacity as determined by the team. The full costs based on scheduled capacity would be used to book accounting transactions and prepare the financial statements, keeping the accountants happy. The costs net of excess capacity could be used for decision-making purposes.

If the project team moves in this direction, it is important that users be trained on how to use the cost information. In the long run, a company must recover all its costs to be profitable. If the company cannot make use of its excess capacity, then it must reduce its managed and committed capacity costs over time to improve its profitability.

YIELD

Yield is a measure of process efficiency. In contrast to capacity, *yield* represents the output that can be produced given a fixed level of input. Input is usually defined as something tangible: a key ingredient, a component, or a document type that is entered into the process. Yield is calculated using the following formula: output ÷ input. A simple example from the service sector will illustrate the concept of yield.

Suppose you work in a personal finance company. You may want to estimate your yield on loan applications by dividing the number of loans approved by the number of loan applications submitted. Suppose during a three-month period you receive 10,000 loan applications, of which only 3,000 are approved. The 3,000 approved loan applications represent a yield factor of 30 percent (3,000 approved applications ÷ 10,000 loan applications = 30%). This number can be very useful for planning and control purposes, in addition to calculating the cost per approved loan.

In manufacturing, the yield calculation may be a little more complex and will probably be based on tests performed during the product development stage. For discrete manufacturers, the calculation of yield is fairly straightforward and will usually be based on a key component. For example, if you input 100 printed circuit boards into an assembly operation, you would expect to get 100 finished products at the end of the operation, a 100 percent yield. However, these types of manufacturers often set yields below 100 percent to provide for unavoidable damage or breakage that might occur during the production process. *Process manufacturers* generally have an expected level of output for each formulation based on a key ingredient.[15] This yield is usually obtained through test trials conducted during the product development process. Examples of yields in different types of industries are shown in Figure 6.7. Sometimes the yield calculation will require the conversion from one unit of measure to another, such as from kilograms or pounds to units. In these situations, a conversion factor should be provided as part of the yield calculation.

Typically, a process will have more than one yield. The *theoretical yield* is the maximum good output for a particular process based on a fixed level of input and the established process design. The theoretical yield represents 100 percent. The *standard yield* is the expected good output based on a fixed level of input and targeted process efficiency. Process efficiency can be determined based on historical experience, test trials under normal operating conditions, or through a formal engineering study. It is usually expressed as a percentage of the theoretical yield. The *actual yield* is the actual output obtained from the process and is also expressed as a percentage of the theoretical yield.

Yield is an important concept in any costing exercise because it can have a significant impact on unit costs. Let us return to our personal finance company. Suppose the industry average ratio of loan applications to approved loans is 60 percent. Management decides to use this figure as the theoretical yield or 100 percent. The standard yield, based on three months of data, would be 50 percent (3,000 ÷ 6,000). Suppose the company incurs $300,000 of labor and overhead costs to process the 10,000 loan applications. The cost per approved loan would be $100 per loan (300,000 ÷ 3,000). Now suppose that through a new marketing campaign,

Figure 6.7 Example of Yields in Different Industries

Industry	Input	Output
Baked goods	Pounds of flour	Pounds of bread
Pharmaceutical	Active ingredient in kilos	Finished product in kilos
Distilled spirits	Tons of molasses	Proof-gallons of alcohol
Utilities	Pounds of carbon	Kilowatt-hours
Financial services	Loan applications	Approved loans
Insurance	Insurance quotes	Policies purchased

management can increase the standard yield from 50 percent to 80 percent. The cost per loan would be reduced dramatically to $62.50.[16]

A similar situation occurs in manufacturing. Pentox is a pharmaceutical company that produces an anxiety-reduction tablet called Pentoxin. The theoretical yield for this product is 2 million tablets; the standard yield is 1.7 million tablets. Figure 6.8 shows the cost calculations of Pentoxin on a batch and per-unit basis. While yield does not affect the total costs of the batch, it has a significant impact on the unit cost calculation, $25.00 versus $21.25 per thousand tablets. *The difference of $3.75 per thousand tablets represents costs that will never be recovered through sales.* If the company had produced the theoretical yield instead of the standard, it would have been able to recover $6,375 of costs per batch through incremental sales.[17] If the company produces 1,000 batches of Pentoxin a year, this number translates into $6,375,000 per year that will go directly to the bottom line.

Figure 6.8 Manufacturing Cost per Batch and per Unit Pentoxin

Total Costs per Batch	
Materials	$29,750
Labor	2,125
Overhead	10,625
Total manufacturing costs per batch	**$42,500**
Yield (in thousands of tablets)	
Theoretical	2,000.0
Standard	1,700.0
Standard yield factor (1,700 ÷ 2000)	85%
Unit Cost (in thousands of tablets)	
Theoretical	$ 21.25
Standard	$ 25.00
Cost improvement opportunity ($25.00 – $21.25)	$ 3.75

The determination of the yield factor is a critical step in the costing process. If the yield factor is not correct, costs will be inaccurate. Team members should not take yield factors as a given, particularly if they are provided by a support area that is not part of the cost redesign project. The team should ask probing questions to the provider of this information:

- How were the yields developed? Were they based on historical data, the yields of similar products, or the opinion of an expert?
- What assumptions underlie the yield calculation?
- If the yield factor was based on a series of test runs, how large was the sample size? You will probably feel more confident on the reliability of the number if they tell you the sample size was 20 versus 2 trials.
- How does the yield factor compare to the historical data?
- What is the variability of the data?

The answers to these questions will allow the team to determine the reliability and accuracy of the information provided. If the information seems unreliable, the team should work with the responsible areas to obtain more accurate data.

TIME STANDARDS

As mentioned in Chapter 5, time standards are a basic building block of many cost systems. Time standards measure how long it takes to complete a process or activity when working under a particular set of conditions. They are typically set in terms of labor hours (or their equivalent) for people-driven processes and machine hours for equipment-driven processes. The total standard process time can also be a combination of labor and machine standards for a series of related activities. Suppose an operator is in charge of a check-sorting operation. Although the machine sorts the checks, there are several activities carried out by the employee at the front and back end of the process. The standard process time per check should include the labor time involved in these front- and back-end activities and the machine time involved in physical check sorting itself.

Time standards are usually developed by industrial engineers who have formal training in how to set physical standards of performance. These standards are used to benchmark operations, improve productivity, increase service levels, and reduce costs. They are also used for headcount and capacity planning and are often the basis for assigning the labor and overhead costs to a product or service. These standards are established by determining the time required to complete an operation. In setting these standards, it is important not only to time the operation, but also to take into account the other factors that might influence the effectiveness with which an employee or a machine can perform a particular task. These factors include the facilities layout, the condition of the equipment, maintenance, the quality of the materials, and employee training.

Time standards are set using work measurement techniques.[18] *Work measurement* determines the time required for a qualified worker to perform a task working at a given pace. Work measurement differs from *method study*, which records and examines the work involved in performing a particular task in order to make improvements. Method study is concerned with eliminating unnecessary movements of workers or materials and substituting good methods for poor ones in order to make improvements in how the work is done. Work measurement, by contrast, is concerned with minimizing unproductive time—the time in which no value-added work is being performed. In an ideal world, method study should precede work measurement, although this is often not the case.

Common work measurement techniques include time studies, work sampling, and estimating.[19] *Time study* is the traditional method used by industrial engineers to set standards. It involves dividing the process being studied into its basic elements and measuring the time it takes to complete each task. This method is most appropriate for processes that have relatively short cycle times and a large number of repetitive operations. Some variations of the time study method include standard data and predetermined time standards.[20]

Work sampling or *activity analysis* involves making sufficient observations of an employee's activities to determine the relative amount of time this person spends on the various activities associated with the process or task at hand. The primary objective of work sampling is to establish how much of the workday is spent performing different types of work. This method is most appropriate for non-repetitive tasks that have long cycle times such as maintenance, material handling, and quality control, among others. One of my clients used this method to set standards in its manufacturing operations because the unstructured nature of its processes did not lend itself well to the use of time studies.

Another simple work measurement technique is *estimating*. Estimating is most appropriate in situations where the time values are not required in great detail such as long-cycle work and where aggregate measurement data are used for planning and control purposes. There are several types of estimating techniques. All estimating techniques rely on the judgment and experience of the person determining the estimates. *Structured estimating* uses the experience of the estimator, but imposes a structure and discipline on the estimating process so that it produces more reliable results. *Analytical estimating* combines the use of estimates and standard data. It breaks down jobs into basic elements and then estimates or measures each one. This method is based on the premise that errors in individual times will be random and will compensate for one another. Therefore, the result when all elements are added together will be an overall time within satisfactory limits. *Comparative estimating* involves the identification and measurement of "benchmark" jobs. These jobs have a well-defined work content that will be used to compare all other jobs to be measured. Comparative estimating is best suited for long-cycle, nonrepetitive work such as maintenance.

Regardless of the actual method used, the team should understand how certain issues are handled in the development of the time standards since they will directly affect the outcome of this process. These issues are discussed in the following sections.

Rating Job Performance

Industrial engineers have typically defined time standards for labor-driven activities as "the time required by an *average worker*, working at a *normal* pace, to complete a specific task using a prescribed method." [Emphasis added][21] Two ambiguous parts of this definition must be clarified in the development of the time standards methodology: who in the organization represents the "average worker" and what is considered a "normal" pace. The frontline supervisor should be able to identify the average worker. The normal pace is an average because no individual can maintain a consistently steady pace for an entire eight-hour shift.

Rating involves comparing the actual work being performed with the analyst's definition of normal pace and quantifying this performance accordingly. Usually, the normal pace is set as the base, or 100 percent. The performance of an individual, which will be used as the basis for the time standards, is adjusted up or down according to the rater's concept of normal. A fast employee might be rated at 110 percent and a slow employee at 80 percent. An effective rating system requires that all analysts consistently apply the same basic performance standard in their measurements. Therefore, any individuals involved in the rating process should be trained so that the ratings are consistent from one analyst to another and are representative of the overall process.

Allowances

Labor standards usually provide an allowance for personal fatigue and delay, known as a *PFD allowance.* The PFD allowance is usually expressed as a percentage of the standard time and is added to the time allowed for the specific task being measured. The allowance differs from company to company and may even differ from one work area to another. It should consider factors relating to the work conditions, the repetitiveness of the task, the physical or mental effort required, and the position in which the worker performs the task. Although the International Labour Office has not adopted any standards relating to the determination of allowances, this aspect of work study has been the subject of extensive research. Various organizations have developed their own recommendations and methodology for the calculation of these allowances.[22] Whether the team uses a systematic approach or a manager's best judgment, it should understand how the PFD allowances were established and should ensure that they are reasonable for each operation under evaluation.

Breaks

Many companies provide their employees with a paid break every four hours worked. How the team accounts for breaks is an important decision in setting time standards. Breaks can be deducted from the total labor hours available per employee or included in the time standard for a particular process. If the process shuts down during the employee breaks, this time can be deducted from the total labor hours available per employee and total process hours available per shift. This treatment would not affect the time standards for the operation, but would affect the number of employees and the number of hours required to complete the operation. The inclusion of breaks as part of the labor utilization calculation will be discussed later on in this chapter.

An alternative treatment is to add breaks to the standard time required to perform the operation. In this situation, the standard times will be higher, but the labor hours available should also be higher. The end result in both situations should be similar. If, however, employees are scheduled to relieve one another during breaks so that the operation never stops, then the inclusion of breaks as part of the standard time is not appropriate because there is no interruption of the workflow.

Equipment Reliability

Time standards for machine-paced operations are set in a similar manner to labor standards, except that the equipment manufacturer usually establishes the maximum operational parameters for the machine. It is within these parameters that the time standards are set using the process specifications initially established by product development. Initial time standards are usually adjusted based on actual experience and should consider equipment reliability. Suppose the process specifications require a packaging line to run at 300 bottles per minute (bpm). The packaging operators have found that running the equipment at this speed produces excessive amounts of defective units due to the product design. Through trial and error, they have discovered that they can significantly reduce this waste by decreasing the speed to 250 bpm. In this type of situation, the team may choose to use the speed of 250 bpm as the basis for setting the time standard versus the theoretical speed of 300 bpm. Now let us further suppose that the reliability rate for this machine is 80 percent; in other words, it is only available for production, on average, 6.4 hours per shift. In this situation, the standard time for this particular product would be set at 200 bottles per minute (250 bpm x 80%). The team may decide, however, that equipment reliability represents an opportunity for process improvement and should not be included in the time standard or the standard cost. There are no right or wrong answers as long as the decision made by the team supports the management philosophy of the organization and is representative of the underlying business process.

Special Allowances

Sometimes, managers may want to include a special allowance in the time standard or adjust the standard cost to account for unavoidable delays that are not included in the PFD allowance. Any special allowance should be closely examined. Why is it needed? Is the allowance truly process-related, or is it a fudge factor to reflect more favorable performance? Any type of allowances will increase cost because more time will be required to complete an operation or process. Therefore, the team should examine the nature and amount of all allowances to ensure that they are realistic and reasonable.

DATA COLLECTION AND ANALYSIS

Standards should be based on sufficient observations so that the values determined can be considered representative of the process or task under evaluation. Most organizations do not have the time or resources to undertake a detailed study of each major process. Therefore, sampling procedures are often used to develop time and yield standards. The sample size is determined by desired level of confidence. The *confidence level* represents the likelihood that the results from the data sample will be representative of the values of the underlying process. The larger the size of the sample, the more representative it becomes of the original group of items under evaluation. Therefore, as sample size increases, the confidence level also increases. Commonly used confidence levels are 90, 95, and 99 percent. The higher the confidence level, the greater assurance you will have that the standard falls within a certain range of values with a set probability. For example, if the yield factor of a particular product has a range of 90 to 95 percent at the 99 percent confidence level, we can state that there is a 99 probability based on the sample data that that the true yield value will fall within this range.

Standards are usually set at the *mean*, a measure of central tendency that represents an average of the sample observations, the historical data points, or the results of several pilot runs. The calculation of the mean for standard setting purposes should exclude *outliers*—data points or observations that are radically different from the rest and are not considered representative of the process. The standard could also be set at the median or the mode. The *median* is another measure of central tendency that represents the middle value in a series of observations arranged in ranked order. In contrast to the mean, the median is not affected by extreme values. The *mode* is the observation that occurs most frequently and is not affected by order or differences of scale. Standards should be set at the mean unless there is a justifiable business reason to set the standard at some other value.

Another important factor in setting standards is the degree of variability in the data. Several statistical measures can be used to describe variability: the range, the standard deviation, and the confidence interval. The *range* is computed as the difference between the maximum value and the minimum value in the data set. For example, a process that has a yield ranging from 85 to 95 percent has more variability than one that has a range of 95 to 98 percent. The range, however, provides no indication of how the data are dispersed around the mean. Here is where another useful statistic becomes handy—the standard deviation. The *standard deviation* provides an indication of how the majority of the data are scattered around the mean. A large standard deviation signifies that the data are spread out from the mean, suggesting a high variability in the output that can be expected from the process or in the time that it takes to complete an activity or task. For example, if you have an activity with an average process time of 5 hours and a standard deviation of 2 hours, your actual times could fluctuate anywhere between 3 and 7 hours 68 percent of the time, significantly affecting your cost, customer service levels, and resource utilization.

An activity with a large standard deviation indicates that there is considerable variability in terms of the time it takes to perform the activity. However, it could also be indicative that the number of observations taken was not sufficient to calculate a reliable estimate. If an activity has a high degree of variability that is not the result of the sampling procedure, it is a prime candidate for process improvement.

Another statistical technique that can be used to describe variability is the confidence interval. The *confidence interval* provides a range of values within which the true population parameter (the yield or time standard) will lie and specifies the likelihood that this interval contains the true value of the population parameter. Similar to the range, the spread of the confidence interval provides an indication of the variability of the process. However, it also provides us with the probability level that the value will fall within this range, a measure that we can use to assess the risk inherent in the standard we choose to set.

High process variability translates into cost volatility. For example, a product or service that has a yield factor with a standard deviation of 2 percent will have more stable costs than one that has a standard deviation of 10 percent. Process variability can also affect customer service levels. If customer due dates are based on time standards that have a large standard deviation, there is a degree of probability that customer expectations will not be met on a regular basis. Therefore, the degree of variability inherent in a process should be carefully analyzed in determining where to set the standard for a particular process.

Monte Carlo simulation is a statistical tool that can be used to evaluate how process variability affects costs and where the team should set standards to meet profitability and customer service objectives (see Appendix C).[23] This tool can help the team understand how the variability of individual activities affects the overall process times, the expected output, and the estimated costs. It can also be used to set the time standards at some point other than the mean to achieve a desired customer service level. Suppose you had an objective of 90 percent on-time delivery. Your process, on average, takes 24 hours from start to finish. If you set the standard at 24 hours, you run the risk of missing your customer service target 50 percent of the time. Therefore, you may want to set your time standard at a higher level to ensure a specific customer service level. Monte Carlo simulation would facilitate this decision process for the team by calculating the expected probability of achieving the on-time delivery goal at different point values. Appendix C provides an example of how Monte Carlo simulations can be used in the standards setting process.

Data collection and analysis involves methods and people. The individuals responsible for data collection and analysis should be trained in standards development and ideally have an industrial engineering background. Some of my clients use engineering students to perform the actual time studies to avoid taxing their internal resources. Be advised, however, that students will require TLC ("tender loving care"). Someone from the project team must be responsible for establishing the data collection guidelines and providing day-to-day supervision for these students. This level of oversight will ensure that the data gets collected according to the definitions and direction established by the team.

LABOR UTILIZATION

Although your processes can be designed at a certain capacity level (i.e., two eight-hour shifts), unless you work in a "lights out" factory, you must ensure that you have the labor resources to run at the desired capacity level. The calculation of total available labor hours allow you to measure your labor capacity and see if it is adequate to cover customer or production demands.

Labor hours available are usually calculated by site, business unit, or work area. Although the results of the calculation may vary within a company, the methodology should be documented and applied consistently across all areas. When a consistent methodology is not used, headcount comparisons among business units may become a meaningless exercise because the manager of each area may be using different assumptions (including the infamous fudge factor) to arrive at a planned headcount number.

The calculation of labor hours available starts with the maximum number of hours that an employee can work during a particular time period, usually a year. In many organizations, this ceiling equates to 2,080 hours (40 hours a week x 52 weeks per year) and is equivalent to the hours paid, assuming that the employee works on a full-time basis. Some organizations, however, require their professional employees to work above 40 hours per week on a regular basis. In these types of organizations, the amount of labor hours available based on a 40-hour week would be too low when you consider paid time off such as holidays, vacations, and other allowances, which will be discussed next. Therefore, the calculation of labor hours should be adjusted to reflect the average workweek of the employee. For example, if the expectation of the firm were that employees work an average of 60 hours per week, then the starting point for the labor hours calculation would be 3,120 hours (60 hours x 52 weeks per year).

Obviously, employees do not work the maximum amount of hours. They take holidays, vacation, get sick, and attend jury duty. These *planned allowances*—the number of hours that an employee typically will not be available for work—should be subtracted from the number of labor hours available. The project team should identify these planned allowances before they embark on a time standards revision because these allowances may affect how time standards are set. For example, should paid breaks be included in the time standard or deducted as a planned allowance from the labor hours available? Some organizations require their employees to change into uniforms and even shower before and after work. Is this a planned allowance or part of the labor standard? There are no right or wrong answers and the team should determine how this issue will be handled within the cost model. At one of my clients, this time was incorporated into the standard before it was considered an integral part of the manufacturing process.

Planned allowances will vary from company to company and may even vary from one business unit to another. They may be established in minutes, hours, days, or as a percentage of total hours. Eventually all planned allowances get converted to hours per time period regardless of how they are set. Typically, planned allowances include the following categories:

○ *Holidays.* The number of holidays is set by management policy. All regular, full-time employees are generally paid the same number of holidays per year.

○ *Vacations.* This figure is also set by company policy. However, depending on the average seniority of the employees in an area, it may vary from one business unit to another. If your average employee has worked with the company for 25 years, they will probably be entitled to more vacation days than if the average employee tenure is one year.

○ *Sick leave.* Sick leave is also set by company policy, though in some jurisdictions a minimum amount may be set by law. Because employees usually will not take the full amount of time they are allotted in any particular time period, the average sick leave hours must be determined for the organizational units under evaluation. This number is expressed as a percentage of total hours or as an absolute figure.

○ *Breaks.* Many companies provide employees with a short break after working a set number of hours. This break should be subtracted from the labor hours available if it is not included in the time standard. The calculation of this allowance is trickier than the ones described previously, because an employee takes breaks only on those days she is working. Therefore, the calculation should be based on workdays and exclude holidays, vacations, sick leave, and any other paid time off.

○ *Meetings.* This category provides for regularly scheduled meetings that disrupt the production or service delivery process. Some companies have regularly scheduled meetings with employees once a month or a quarter. These hours should be subtracted from the hours available.

○ *Training.* When employees are in training, they are unavailable for work, unless of course, it is on-the-job training. A manager should estimate the amount of time employees will be involved in training and therefore be unavailable for work.

○ *Other allowances.* Every company has its own particularities, which may affect the productive labor hours of their employees. For example, some companies require that their employee change into uniforms or shower as they enter and leave the work area and pay employees for the time involved in these activities. This time must also be subtracted from the labor hours available.

LaborHrs_Available.xls is an Excel template that can be used as a basis for calculating the labor hours available in your organization. This file is available at *www.wiley.com/go/costsystems* (see "About the Web Site" in the front section of this book). You may modify this template to take into consideration the particularities of your environment. Figure 6.9 shows an example of this calculation.

The labor hours available calculation is a useful number for planning, forecasting, and budgeting your labor resources. Let us suppose you are the manager of restaurant, which operates 16 hours per day, 360 days per year. You have six workstations that need to be covered at all times in order to properly service your customers. What is the minimum number of employees that will be required to run this operation? Assume the labor hours available per employee are those calculated in Figure 6.9. The number of employees required would be calculated as follows:

Figure 6.9 How to Calculate Labor Hours Available

Description	Time Allowed	Unit of Measure	Total Hours	For information purposes only	
Total hours paid per year			2080	Total hours paid:	
Planned allowances				Per day	8
Holidays	5.0	days	40	Per week	40
Vacations	10.0	days	80	Per year	2080
Breaks*	0.5	hrs/day	120	Days paid	260
Sick leave	42.0	hrs/yr	42	Days available	240
Meetings	1.0	hrs/month	12		
Training	2.0	hrs/month	24		
Subtotal planned allowances			318		
Total available labor hours			1,762		
% Utilization			85%		

* Breaks will be the same number of minutes per day for all areas.
  Breaks = Available workdays x hours per day
  Available workdays = Days paid less holidays, vacations, and sick leave

Total labor hours required	34,560	(16 hours/day **x** 360 days
		x 6 workstations)
Hours available per employee	1,762	
Number of employees required	19.61	(34,560 hours ÷ 1,762 hours)

Obviously, it is impossible to have 19.61 employees. So how do you handle this 0.61? The answer to this question depends on your perspective—an operations manager will probably round up to 20 employees; a finance manager will probably round down to 19. At 20 employees, you will have some labor cushion, while at 19, you will need to work overtime or hire temporary employees to meet your service requirements. The issue becomes a judgment call by management.

The labor hours available calculation is commonly used in manufacturing organizations to plan the direct labor headcount. It often becomes a battle between the accountants and the line managers. Accountants will typically multiply the labor standards in the system by the forecasted volumes to determine the total labor hours required and calculate the expected headcount figure for the area. This number is usually considerably lower than the line manager's estimate. Line managers will argue that the time standards do not provide for tasks that are performed by production personnel such as material handling or data entry and do not consider that some production lines require a fixed number of employees per shift, no matter how many hours the line is actually running.

Although it is often difficult to reconcile the calculated headcount to the actual or budgeted headcount in a particular area, significant differences should be analyzed and resolved by the team. These differences may be caused by inaccurate time standards, process variability, special projects, or support activities that were not included in the standard but are performed by direct labor personnel. The calculation should be viewed as a tool to raise labor utilization issues and plan headcount. It should not be used to cast in stone the number of employees required in a particular area. This tunnel vision might result in the proverbial "penny-wise, pound foolish" that will affect your ability to service the customer down the road.

COST TYPES

So far, we have focused primarily on operational issues. We now turn our focus to cost issues. One important decision for the team is what types of costs to use in their costing models. Costs can be calculated using actual, standard, last, or forecasted costs as explained next.

Actual Costs

Actual costs are based on the current costs of the resources consumed. They are based on actual usage and input prices versus using a predetermined standard. Many information systems have the capability to track the actual costs of labor, materials, and overhead and calculate actual unit costs accordingly. In these systems, the actual cost is generally recalculated based on a weighted average each time a raw material, subassembly, or intermediate product is received into inventory.

Actual costing systems have the advantage of providing current cost information for decision-making purposes. While there are no cost variances to be explained, actual costs should be compared against a benchmark to ensure that significant process inefficiencies are highlighted and corrective action is taken. One possible benchmark is the expected cost. *Expected costs* are based on materials quantity standards, time standards, and the most current costs available for materials. Labor and overhead costs are assigned to products or services using a predetermined rate based on actual costs, which is updated regularly every three to six months as deemed by management. The use of expected costs allows a company to manage the business using the most current cost information available and at the same time, have a benchmark to measure performance and identify cost improvement opportunities.

Standard Costs

Standard costs are expected costs that serve as goals to be achieved and are expressed on a per-unit basis. They are based on materials quantity standards, time standards, and a forecasted cost of labor, materials, and other inputs for a particular time period. The difference between standard and expected costs is that standard costs are usually set once a year during the budgeting process and are seldom revised. Unless there is a significant difference between the actual and the standard cost or there is a radical change in the business, the standard cost will remain in place for the entire budget period, typically one year.

Standard cost systems are useful as a planning tool for budgeting or forecasting purposes. However, as a control and performance measurement tool, they have significant drawbacks. One is the lack of flexibility to revise costs to reflect changing business conditions. Because standards are usually set once a year, these systems are in direct conflict with current management thinking that emphasizes flexible processes and adaptability to the environment. Another major drawback is the complexity of standard cost systems. Generally, accountants design these systems without considering the needs of line personnel. They are accounting, not operations-focused systems. *Variance analysis*, which attempts to explain the difference between actual and standard costs, also adds a layer of complexity to the record-keeping process that makes it difficult to understand and analyze cost behavior. Accountants spend a substantial amount of time and effort analyzing and explaining cost variances in their financial reports at the expense of helping line managers identify problems and opportunities on a more real time basis. Finally, standard costs may not be representative of the actual costs incurred and may steer managers in the wrong direction. Although actual costs can be calculated under a standard cost system, cost variances are commonly reported as an aggregate number and are rarely used to calculate the actual costs per unit on a regular basis.

Standard cost systems can be a valuable tool for organizations that operate in a stable environment and have not implemented sophisticated computer applications to help run the business. However, operations control should take place on the production floor or the service frontline not in accounting. Cost analysts should spend less time analyzing cost variances and more time helping managers understand their cost structure and how their decisions affect the financial performance of the organization.

Last Costs

Last costs represent the most current costs available for the resources consumed in the manufacturing or service delivery process. The use of this valuation method is appropriate when the last cost most accurately represents the actual or projected cost of the item. In situations where the cost of an item shows a consistent upward or downward trend, the last cost may be more accurate than the average actual or standard cost.

Forecasted Costs

Forecasted or *projected costs* are estimated future costs based on the best available information. These costs are appropriate when estimating costs for future time periods. Projected costs can incorporate changes to materials quantity standards, labor requirements, and input prices over time. They are appropriate for planning and forecasting exercises as well as decision analysis situations.

Considerations in Choosing the Appropriate Cost Type

The cost type will depend on the purpose for which the cost is being developed. Actual and standard costs are used primarily for planning, measurement, and control; last and forecasted costs are used mainly for planning and decision analysis. Often, corporate financial policy will dictate the type of cost that will be used. If your company uses a standard cost system, you will probably have to use standard costs as the basis for your cost system. Small to medium-sized companies usually have more flexibility in this area than subsidiaries of large, multinational corporations. In addition to corporate policy, the choice of a cost type also depends on other factors such as the availability of information, systems support, organizational maturity, and labor resources. For example, a company that does not have time standards in place would find little value-added in setting up a standard cost system. A good cost system, however, should incorporate flexibility allowing costs to be calculated using the most appropriate cost type for the particular decision or situation at hand.

COSTING METHODS

Most organizations use a full cost absorption system to calculate the cost of their products or services. However, this traditional costing approach has been highly criticized over the past 20 years for its inability to produce relevant information for decision-making purposes. As a result, other costing methodologies such as activity-based costing and throughput accounting have evolved as alternatives to the traditional full cost method.

These costing paradigms are not necessarily breakthrough ideas but represent an evolution of accounting concepts that have been around for decades. *Activity-based costing (ABC)* is a full cost approach. Throughput accounting shares many similarities with the traditional concepts of *direct* or *variable costing*. The difference in these new approaches is their ability to tie cost information to the business processes of the organization and herein lay their value-added contribution to the management accounting knowledge base.

Activity-based costing (ABC) focuses on the activities that are performed in an organization. It assumes that activities consume resources and traces costs to products or services through the activities that they require. Although it is often not cost-effective to implement an ABC system in an organization, the analysis of activities and the resources that they consume in relation to the products or services can be very useful to highlight problem areas and identify cost-improvement opportunities. It can also assist managers in developing a better understanding of the demand that products and services create on the activities of the organization and hence on its resource utilization.

ABC focuses primarily on indirect labor and overhead costs. It will not affect the calculation of materials costs because these are developed based on standard or estimated quantities and are unaffected by how costs are assigned to different activities. Direct labor costs may or may not be affected, depending on what types of employees are included in the calculation of the labor rate, based on the activity analysis.

Activity analysis and cost assignment using ABC can be used in conjunction with standard, actual, or forecasted costs. A detailed description and explanation of ABC is beyond the scope of this book. However, many good books have been written on this subject, some of which are included in the reference section of this book.

Another costing method is *throughput accounting (TA)*, which is based on Eli Goldratt's Theory of Constraints (TOC). As explained in an earlier section of this chapter, TOC takes a systemic view of the organization, where the performance of the overall system depends on the interrelationship of the elements that compose it. It is based on the premise that any process has at least one constraint that will limit its throughput and, therefore, its ability to create value. *Throughput (T)* is defined as the sales less totally variable costs. *Totally variable costs* increase or decrease in direct proportion to the output sold. Materials are an excellent example of totally variable costs.

TOC concerns itself with three measurements: throughput (T), investment (I), and operating expenses (OE). We have already defined throughput. *Investment (I)* is the money invested in inventory or those items that the system intends to sell. *Operating expense (OE)* is defined as the money spent to convert investment into throughput. Throughput accounting uses these three TOC measurements to build accounting statements and provide cost information. It does not allocate labor and overhead costs to individual products or services, but manages these costs in the aggregate. It also does not classify costs as fixed or semivariable and is concerned only with totally variable costs. Throughput accounting is an evolution of *variable costing*. In variable costing, fixed overhead costs are not included in inventory and are expensed to the income statement in the period incurred. Throughput accounting takes this one step further by expensing all costs that are not classified as totally variable. Throughput—the difference between sales and totally variable costs (materials)—is a progression of the concept of contribution margin in variable costing—the difference between sales and variable costs.

Throughput accounting, like variable costing, has serious limitations in the real world as a standalone tool. It does not consider how a product or service may burden support areas (e.g., quality control in a pharmaceutical company) until the point that it becomes the system constraint, at which point the organization may already be on its knees. It does not consider how a product consumes its support resources, which perhaps could be used more productively by the organization to create value. However, throughput accounting is a useful tool in situations of over or under capacity where full costing can lead managers astray. In addition, the simplicity of its conceptual framework provides managers with a sense of focus and direction without complex calculations and analysis. The answer to three simple questions can guide day-to-day decisions: Will it increase throughput? Will it decrease inventory? Will it result in a reduction of operating expenses? An affirmative answer to any of these questions will probably result in a net improvement to the bottom line of the organization. When combined with activity-based costing, it becomes a very powerful tool to gain insights into the business and identify opportunities for cost savings and process improvements.

SUMMARY

Some companies take the operational parameters that underlie their cost system and cost calculation methodology as a given. They do not take the time to challenge the fundamental assumptions that are used to develop costs or question how the costs themselves are being calculated. In my experience, accountants sometimes change numbers or information submitted by line managers without their knowledge to make the costs "look good" without understanding the business implications of the changes that they are making. However, line managers sometimes submit information that is inaccurate or incomplete, not fully understanding how this affects the reported costs of the products, services, or operational units and the business strategies of the organization.

This chapter has described some of the issues that will be confronted by the team as they proceed in the design process. The advantage of using a cross-functional project team is that members can share their functional expertise and discuss the advantages and disadvantages of a particular approach from different perspectives. Although the final resolution may involve some type of compromise or trade-off, the important point is that these issues have been discussed and agreed upon by the team. Once they agree on a particular approach, it creates a common language and a shared vision on how costs will be calculated, reported, and managed. The payback of this process is immense as better operational and cost information is available for management decision making.

ENDNOTES

1. See Richard B. Chase and Nicholas J. Aquilano, *Production and Operations Management: A Life Cycle Approach* (Homewood, IL: Richard D. Irwin, Inc., 1989), and Carol J. McNair and Richard

Vangermeersch, *Total Capacity Management: Optimizing at the Operational, Tactical, and Strategic Levels* (New York: St. Lucie Press, 1998).

2. Thomas Klammer, ed., *Capacity Measurement and Improvement: A Manager's Guide to Evaluating and Optimizing Capacity Productivity* (Burr Ridge, IL: Irwin Professional Publishing, 1996).

3. Throughput, in TOC terminology, is defined as the sales less totally variable costs.

4. This is the conceptual underpinning of TOC, espoused by Eliyahu Goldratt in his book, *The Goal* (1984).

5. Anne E. Gray and James Leonard, "Capacity Analysis: Sample Problems," Harvard Business School Note, #9-606-058 (Massachusetts: Harvard Business School Publishing, 1995), 8.

6. Theoretical capacity = 24 hours per day x 360 days per year = 8,640 hours.

7. Practical capacity = 24 hours per day x 260 days per year = 6,240 hours.

8. Available capacity =16 hours per day x 260 days per year = 4,160 hours.

9. Budgeted production volume expressed in process hours = budgeted units of output x standard process hours per unit = 60,000 units x 0.05 hours per unit = 3,000 hours.

10. "Practices and Techniques of Measuring the Cost of Capacity," Statement of Management Accounting, Statement No. 4Y, March 1996.

11. *Semivariable costs* are those that have a fixed and variable component. Maintenance, electricity, and water are examples of semivariable costs. *Step-fixed costs* are those that increase in discrete steps beyond a certain level of output. These costs remain fixed within an established range and they increase in a step-like fashion when the output exceeds this range. An example of a step-fixed cost is indirect labor. When volume increases beyond a certain level, the organization may have to hire line mechanics or quality control technicians even though these employees might not be fully utilized at the new activity levels.

12. Peter B.B. Turney, *Common Cents*, 39-40.

13. Thomas Klammer, ed., *Capacity Measurement and Improvement*, 69–71; Robert S. Kaplan and Robin Cooper, *Cost & Effect* (1997).

14. The $3.44 per invoice is calculated as follows: $2.75 cost ÷ (1 − desired profit margin) = $2.75 ÷ (1 − 0.20) = $2.75 ÷ (0.80) = $3.44.

15. Process manufacturers produce like items in lots or batches that are indistinguishable from each other. Some examples of process manufacturers include baked goods, paper, chemicals, and soft drinks.

16. This amount is calculated by dividing the total labor and over-head costs of $300,000 by the new standard yield, which is 4,800 [theoretical yield = 6,000 x 80% = 4,800 standard yield).

17. This number is calculated as follows: (theoretical − standard yield) x theoretical unit cost = (2,000.0 − 1,700.0 = 300.0) x $21.25 = $6,375 per batch. Another way to calculate this number is by multiplying the standard yield by the cost improvement opportunity per unit [1,700 units x 3.75 per unit = $6,375 per batch].

18. George Kanawaty, *An Introduction to Work Study*, 4th ed. (Geneva, Switzerland: International Labour Office, 1992), 243.

19. For more information on work measurement methods, see Lawrence S. Aft, *Work Measurement & Methods Improvement* (New York: John Wiley & Sons, Inc., 2000), and George Kanawaty, *An Introduction to Work Study*, 4th ed. (Geneva, Switzerland: International Labour Office, 1992).

20. *Standard data systems* organize standard times from a number of related tasks into a database that is used to determine time standards. The time standards are initially developed by skilled personnel using direct measurement. Allowances for personal fatigue and delay are usually added after the standards are constructed with the standard data system. *Predetermined time standards* are standard data systems that are used when it is not feasible to time operations or use a company-developed database to develop standards. These systems have been designed to fit a variety of

process and product applications and have broad applicability. For more information on these methods, see Aft (2000) and Kanawaty (1992).

21. See Aft (1992), 148.

22. For a detailed example of the tables used to calculate allowances, see Kanawaty (1992), 489, Appendix 3.

23. *Monte Carlo simulation* is a technique that uses random number generation to reproduce alternate scenarios based on certain assumptions as defined by the user. This approach allows users to incorporate variability and risk into their decision model and provides a tool to better understand the probability of specific outcomes and to identify the key variables that are driving the results. Many of us may remember Monte Carlo simulations as a very complex statistical tool. However, advances in computer technology and software applications have made this tool readily accessible and understandable to the average business professional. For more information on this tool, readers are encouraged to visit *www.decisioneering.com.*

7

Cost Systems Setup and Test

This stage begins immediately after the team has preliminarily agreed upon the conceptual design of the cost model. It may run parallel to the system design stage, because the team might still be sorting the costing issues discussed in the prior chapter while gathering data on its processes. This stage may be very intense for some team members, particularly if they are working against a deadline such as the submission of a budget or the start of a new fiscal year.

As discussed in Chapter 3, this stage involves four steps: (1) data gathering, (2) data validation, (3) systems setup, and (4) systems test. In this chapter we will discuss in more detail the specific tasks that must be accomplished in each step. These steps should be performed sequentially to avoid unnecessary rework at a critical stage of the project. Be advised that the team will probably run multiple iterations of the cost model as part of the setup and test process. However, these multiple runs can be minimized if the team ensures that it is working with the best available data.

STEP 1: DATA GATHERING

The data gathering process is a balancing act of time and resources. When resources are not dedicated 100 percent to the project, the day-to-day workload and other pressing priorities often interfere with the team's ability to collect data. In addition, the quality of the existing data also affects the timeframe in which this step can be accomplished. Some organizations already have the basic information required to redesign their cost models, such as an analysis of the business processes, time standards, labor utilization, yields, capacity utilization, and materials quantities. For these types of organizations, the data-gathering stage involves updating the information to reflect the current business conditions. Depending on the resources available and the number of processes or items to be analyzed, this step can take anywhere from three to six months. Other organizations, however, do not have this information readily available, so it must be collected from scratch. In this situation, the data collection can take anywhere from six months to more than a year. For example, at one of my clients, we recorded cycle times and scrap levels for more than 200 different products. In order to validate the data, we collected information for the same product several times and reconciled any significant differences. Data collection for this work area took over a year. Another client had some information available, but not the type of information required by the new cost model design. Therefore, they had to collect this information over a six-month period before we could run the new cost calculations.

The type of information required depends on whether you are a service or manufacturing organization and how you have structured your cost model. You will typically need the following information:

○ *Volume.* The volume levels usually drive the amount of resources required or consumed by the organization. It is the starting point for any budgeting or forecasting exercise and is a critical element to determine capacity utilization and its impact on the cost structure of the organization.

○ *Materials quantities.* This information is a must for manufacturing organizations and will generally be found in the bill of materials, as discussed in Chapter 5. It lists the quantities required of each component or ingredient that is used to manufacture the product. In some service organizations, materials may also represent significant costs. For example, a power generation facility typically consumes a significant amount of carbon or fuel in the production of electricity. Usually these types of organizations will have some type of ratio or standard that establishes the amount of materials input required per unit of output.

○ *Expected output or yield.* For process manufacturers, each product should have an expected or theoretical output for each formulation based on the key ingredient. For discrete manufacturers, this expected output is usually 100 percent of a key component, such as a printed circuit or motherboard. In service organizations, the expected yield represents the expected output of a process based on a fixed level of input. For example, in a mortgage lending company, yield could be expressed as the number of loans approved as a percent of the number of loan applications received or processed.

○ *Yield factor.* This factor will adjust the theoretical or expected output to reflect current or projected operating conditions. A yield factor of 100 percent indicates that 100 percent of the input will be converted into output.

○ *Scrap factor.* This factor will reflect how much materials are lost as a normal part of the process. Typically you will have a scrap or yield factor, but not both. Discrete manufacturers commonly use the scrap factor to recognize expected materials losses resulting from breakage, spillage, equipment failures, and operator errors.

○ *Process parameters.* Process parameters underlie the time standards calculation, particularly for machine-paced operations. They generally describe the cycle time of the process such as bottles or capsules per minute and the number of workers required to run the operation. Process parameters vary significantly from industry to industry. For example, in the injection molding industry, the process parameters would include the number of cavities per mold, the number of operating cavities per mold, in addition to the cycle time, expressed as seconds per shot, and the number of employees required to run a particular machine.

○ *Time standards.* Time standards are determined based on the process parameters, the data collected from a work measurement study, or a combination of both. If the time standards are based on the existing data available in the organization, the team members should ensure that the data are consistent with the system design as agreed upon by the team. Typically, time standards are used to identify areas for process improvements and assign labor and overhead costs.

○ *Capacity.* The team should determine the practical and available capacity of each major business process and how much of this capacity is being utilized. This information can help identify improvements in capacity utilization and is used to isolate the cost of excess capacity in the unit costs.

○ *Labor hours available.* The team should calculate the labor hours available for each major area based on the assumptions agreed upon as part of the system design. Although not a critical element of the cost model, it is used primarily for headcount planning and understanding labor utilization. It provides insight on how the organization is using its labor resources and can highlight opportunities to reduce nonproductive time. This information can be easily linked to costs allowing managers to understand how much unused or underutilized labor resources are costing the organization.

○ *Materials costs.* This cost represents the actual, standard, forecasted, or last cost of the material components or ingredients that are consumed by the product or service. The materials costs usually includes the purchase price of the goods plus other costs such as freight, insurance, royalty payments, sales tax, brokerage fees, and duties. In organizations that have high materials costs, focusing on this area can produce significant cost savings.

○ *Labor and overhead costs.* This information is necessary to calculate the labor and overhead rate that will be used to assign these costs to the items being measured. Usually organizations budget and collect labor and overhead costs by work areas or departments. The team should ensure that the way the organization is currently collecting actual costs is consistent with the system design. New departments may have to be created or existing cost centers may have to be consolidated. Information may have to be reorganized to reflect the proposed departmental cost structure per the cost model design. Typically, labor and overhead costs are based on the budgeted, forecasted, or actual cost figures. The choice of which cost to use will depend on which one best reflects the current business conditions of the organization.

○ *Dedicated resources.* Labor and overhead resources that are dedicated 100 percent to a specific product, product family, service, or customer should only be charged to those items that consume them. Therefore, the analysis of labor and overhead costs discussed previously also involves the identification of dedicated resources. The cost of these resources should be excluded from the calculation of the general labor and overhead rate that will be applied across a broad range of products or services.

Figure 7.1 provides a checklist of the typical data that will be required to perform a costing exercise and where the data can usually be found in the organization. As the required data become available, the team can proceed to the next step—the validation of the data collected.

STEP 2: DATA VALIDATION

As the data are gathered, they should be validated by the team. Data validation can be done in several ways:

○ *Comparisons with currently available information.* The new or revised data upon which the cost model calculations will be based can be compared to existing information available in the organization. How significant are the differences? Do they make sense in light of the cost model design? Sometimes the design of the new system is so radically different that it is not possible to perform any type of comparisons with existing information—either because the data were not previously available or were collected using totally different assumptions. In these situations, the data validation will rely more on the collective know-how of the team members and other experts in the organization. In addition, the team can use process or product comparisons with the new information collected to validate the data.

○ *Product comparisons.* This type of comparison involves comparing the data gathered for one product with another to ensure that the differences can be explained by the nature of the business process or the type of product. For example, suppose you are a manufacturer of baked goods. You notice that the time standard for baking one type of cake is twice the time standard of a similar product. You should understand what characteristics of the product or process account for this time difference. If you cannot explain the

Figure 7.1 Checklist of Typical Information Required to Calculate Costs and Possible Sources Where the Information Can Be Found

Type of Data	Possible Sources of Information
Volume	• Budget or forecast system • Order processing system • Inventory management or production control • Master Production Schedule (MPS) • Materials Requirements Planning (MRP) • Planning personnel
Material quantity standards	• Bill of Materials (BOM) file • Product specifications sheet
Yield	• Bill of Materials (BOM) file • Item Master file • Process specification sheet • Engineering or operations personnel
Yield factor	• Bill of Materials file (BOM) • Item Master file • Process specification sheet • Planning, purchasing, engineering or operations personnel
Scrap factor	• Bill of Materials (BOM) file • Item Master file • Planning, purchasing, engineering or operations personnel
Process parameters	• Process or product specification sheet • Planning, purchasing, engineering, or operations personnel • Data collection system
Time standards	• Routing file • Engineering studies • Production personnel • Equipment specifications
Capacity	• Operations personnel
Labor hours available	• Typically calculated by finance or accounting personnel based on the assumptions agreed upon by the team.
Materials costs	• Item Master file • Purchasing personnel • Suppliers
Labor and overhead costs	• Budget • General ledger • Forecasts
Dedicated resources	• Operations personnel • Fixed asset ledger • Process flowcharts

difference, the time standard for the product should be reexamined to ensure it was properly established.

○ *Review with experts.* The data should be reviewed with the experts in the organization to ensure that they are reliable and accurate. Time standards, in particular, should be validated with the line managers responsible for the work area.

○ *Industry or company benchmarks.* The team might find that certain information is available from industry studies or other sites within the company that can be used as a reality check for the data collected. Sometimes information from inside the company is more difficult to obtain than an industry benchmark because locations compete against one another for new products or customers.

○ *Team review.* Team members should review all the data that will underlie their cost calculations as they become available. Each team member brings a unique perspective to the project. The review of data outside their particular field of expertise may trigger the identification of issues and opportunities that had not been previously thought of. You do not want team members during the system test stage to question the validity of the data simply because they did not have a chance to review the data beforehand.

After data validation, the team is ready to start creating templates or setting up their system applications to perform the cost calculations.

STEP 3: SYSTEMS SETUP

In this step, the team will enter the information gathered in Step 2 into whatever application they will use to calcuate their costs. Hopefully, the team has given some thought to their company's existing system applications as part of the design stage. You do not want to uncover at this stage that the current systems application is totally unsuited for running the revised cost model.

However, the team might have to devise a workaround to the system to get it to calculate costs according to the system design. Because the costing application is generally integrated with operational subsystems such as the Item Master, the Bill of Materials, and the Routing file, the team must ensure that in the process of developing a workaround, it has not inadvertently affected how manufacturing or service personnel enter and report information. The system applications may cost products perfectly, but you might not be able to close orders or report production. If the new cost system requires a change in the data entry or reporting procedures, these should be identified and discussed with the personnel involved. You do not want surprises on the day the system goes live!

Some organizations do not have an integrated systems solutions to cost their products or services. These organizations typically use spreadsheet or standalone programs to develop their unit costs and analyze cost information. However, the use of a spreadsheet program has several drawbacks, as will be discussed in more detail in Chapter 9. Spreadsheet programs become particularly cumbersome if the organization has a large number of items that must be costed. Standalone programs are more efficient than spreadsheets, but also involve risks for the organization. These will also be discussed in Chapter 9.

During this step, the team might uncover issues that require them to rethink the conceptual design of the model. It is perfectly acceptable to rethink some aspects of the system design based on new information or insights. As I have repeatedly mentioned throughout this book, the design of a cost system is an iterative process. If the team has done its homework in Steps 1 and 2, any additional issue uncovered should not require a major overhaul to the system design.

The systems setup can be time-consuming and cumbersome depending on the size and complexity of the organization. It might require pulling in additional resources from other areas or hiring temporary personnel to enter the data into the system. This step is one where top management commitment is vital. If the entire management team is not committed to the project, managers may not be willing to shift priorities and reassign resources at this critical point. If the team is working toward a deadline, this lack of commitment and resources may bring the project to a standstill.

STEP 4: SYSTEMS TEST

In this final step, the team calculates the unit costs and reviews the results. This review usually results in changes to the systems setup or the correction of errors in the data that underlie the cost calculations. Sometimes, the preliminary cost run is an eye-opener for the operations personnel. One client developed the time standards for all major tests performed by the quality control (QC) laboratory, determined the number of tests required for each product, and used this information to assign the costs of the lab to the products. This exercise led to the identification of several products where reduced testing was possible or where the QC tests could be conducted in a more efficient manner, lowering the total product costs. At another client, the manufacturing managers stared in disbelief at the revised costs and argued that there was something wrong with the costing methodology. When we examined the operational parameters, *which they had provided*, the revised costing system was providing an accurate representation of the business process as defined. They realized that in order to be competitive in the marketplace, they had to focus on the efficiency of their manufacturing process, lowering cycle times, setup times, and scrap.

The systems test also involves ensuring that the systems applications work as described in the systems documentation. Although this might seem an oxymoron, I repeatedly encounter systems where the documentation states one thing and the system does another. Sometimes, it is a flag that must be set by the user or the system administrator, which was not obvious in reading the documentation; other times, it is a bug that requires a programming fix. *Turnkey applications* are less likely to require programming changes than custom or in-house applications.[1] My experience with turnkey systems is that most of the programming effort occurs in the development of user reports to extract information from the system. Many turnkey systems now incorporate query functions that provide simple and easy-to-use report-writing capabilities.

During the system test, the team must also document and test any new accounting and operational procedures that will affect how actual data are collected and reported. These procedures might involve data entry, report generation, or the preparation of accounting entries. At the end of the system test, the team should be ready to go live with the new costing system with minimal implementation problems.

IMPORTANCE OF DOCUMENTATION

At the end of the systems setup and test stage, you should thoroughly document the conceptual framework and the major cost elements, and should provide a detailed description of how the new cost system works. *I cannot emphasize enough the importance of documentation as a final step in the development process.* The preparation of a cost manual ensures consistency and continuity in the development of cost information as people change jobs or leave the organization. It also provides a training manual for current and new employees to understand how cost information is prepared and reported.

The specific contents of the documentation will vary from company to company. It usually contains the following information:

○ *General information.* This section provides general information about the cost system redesign project—when it was undertaken, who was involved, and what date it was implemented. It is important to document the composition of the project team in this section. This information adds credibility to the project and will clearly identify the members of the project team should questions arise in the future.

○ *Project objectives and deliverables.* This section should clearly define the purpose of the new cost system, the project scope, and the expected results.

○ *The conceptual framework.* This section outlines the theoretical underpinnings of the new system. It should provide an overview of the business processes and key technologies in each major organizational subunit involved in the production or service delivery process. If possible, flowcharts or diagrams of the process should be included as part of this section. This section should also contain key terms and definitions that were agreed upon by the team and provide the theoretical foundations for many important design and setup decisions.

○ *A description of the costing methodology.* The documentation should explain *in detail* how costs are calculated by the new cost system. I have found the inclusion of a comprehensive example—which clearly references spreadsheets, replicates formulas, and shows the detailed cost calculations—to be very effective. Copies of all spreadsheets and query programs used to extract information should be included as part of this documentation. I learned this the hard way. For one client, we used a number of queries to extract information, which was the basis of the cost model calculations. During the implementation of a major systems upgrade, however, the queries were lost and the client was unable to use the backup tapes to restore the information. Because the client did not have printed copies of the queries, it was forced to reconstruct the reports and retest the whole process. I now recommend to all my clients that they keep a hard copy of all query instructions as well as other key reports as part of the system documentation.

○ *Time standards methodology.* If the organization uses time standards, it is critical to document *from an operational standpoint* how these standards were set. This section should explain the methods used to determine the time standards (work sampling, time studies, expert personnel), the key business assumptions such as how breaks were handled or how machine time was determined, and any other information such as the calculation of the PDF allowance and operator rating that may affect the time calculation. If possible, the preparer of this section should provide a detailed example that walks the reader through the standards-setting process in a simplified manner. This section should be written by the individual or individuals involved in the time standards revision and should be reviewed by the entire project team.

The organization should appoint someone from the project team to remain the custodian of the cost model documentation. This person is charged with the responsibility of updating the documentation as the cost model evolves with changes in the business. My experience is that once the documentation is prepared, it is rarely updated because there is always something in the organization that has a greater priority. As a result, years down the road, the cost model procedures bear little resemblance to the documented practices, even though the conceptual design may remain unchanged. If the keepers of this knowledge leave the organization abruptly, the organization will find itself at risk because no one in the organization has the technical expertise to run the cost model.

I have also encountered the reverse situation—the cost system designers leave the organization and the torch passes on to another individual who understands the mechanics of the model, but not its conceptual underpinnings. As the business evolves, the individual does not make any changes because they do not really understand the operational assumptions that are driving the cost model. In this situation, the cost model rapidly falls into obsolescense.

SUMMARY

The setup and test stage is where the rubber meets the road. It is when the team enters real numbers into a conceptual design and evaluates the reasonableness of the output. Based on the results of their evaluation, the team might decide to change the system design, the project deliverables, the cost terminology, or any other agreement previously made by the team. *Cost system redesign is an iterative process.* At any stage, the team should feel free to go back and question decisions made in a prior stage based on new information. This continual questioning is important to ensure the system supports the strategic objectives in the simplest and most cost-effective manner.

ENDNOTE

1. *Turnkey applications* are information systems applications designed and developed by third-party vendors, which can be customized through the system setup to different types of businesses. Typically, the vendors of these types of systems do not sell the source code; therefore, it is almost impossible to change the fundamental workings of the system except through vendor-supported add-ins or customized programs provided by the vendor.

8

Performance Measurement and Reporting

Performance measures provide the critical link between strategy and execution by providing a mechanism to evaluate and communicate performance against expected results. They bring the planning cycle full loop by supplying management with vital feedback on how well they have executed against their plans. Costs are an important element of any performance measurement system because any actions taken (or not taken) by the organization have financial implications. Cost information allows managers to quantify the cost of the resources consumed in executing organization strategies and determine whether their actions have resulted in an increase or decrease in the economic value of the organization. Cost systems should feed information into the performance measurement systems so that key metrics can be associated with the financial results of the organization.

Many organizations see their cost and performance measurement system as two separate management information systems. Accountants prepare cost reports and financial statements, while line managers report on those key indicators that measure the efficiency and effectiveness of their operations. Sometimes the information provided by one area is inconsistent with that provided by another, creating unnecessary conflict and debate about which is the "correct" number.

In Chapter 2, we discussed performance measures as one of the six elements of an effective cost system. In this chapter, we discuss in more depth what performance metrics can be provided by your cost system and how these can be integrated into a more comprehensive performance management system for management decision-making purposes. We will also discuss management reporting, another key element of an effective cost system. Cost information should be reported in a timely manner and in a user-friendly format in order to prompt the organization to act. Cost system designers should ensure that cost information is integrated into the performance measurement and management reporting system of the organization in a way that furthers the goals of the organization.

WHAT TYPES OF PERFORMANCE MEASURES ARE WE TALKING ABOUT?

Most organizations have some type of performance measurement system to assess organizational performance. In some organizations, these measures are strictly financial in nature—for example, net income, earnings per share, or key financial ratios—while others combine financial and nonfinancial indicators to provide management with a more holistic view of organizational performance. In my experience, organizations have either too many or too few performance measures that are often decoupled from the strategic objectives of the organization. Time and resources are dedicated to preparing reports that lie unread and unused, while critical operational parameters are not measured or managed.

The Institute of Management Accountants (IMA) has identified six key attributes of effective performance measures:[1]

1. *Linked to strategy.* Performance measures should be tied to specific strategic objectives and aligned throughout the organization. They should cascade down the organizational hierarchy to ensure organizational alignment with company objectives.

2. *Actionable.* Managers and employees should have the ability to significantly change or influence the measured results through their actions. The performance measure monitors the effectiveness of their actions in producing the desired results.

3. *Measurable.* Good performance measures can be quantified in a meaningful manner. An adequate mechanism should be in place to gather and report the information in a timely manner.

4. *Simple.* Measures should be straightforward and easy to understand. Their relevance and importance should be readily apparent to all individuals in the organization.

5. *Few.* Performance measures are limited in number. They should contain only those measures needed to direct attention to the appropriate areas. When an organization has too many performance measures, measurement becomes an end in itself. For each measurement in the organization, management should be able to explain how it will affect their actions or influence their decision-making process. Measurement is a means to an end, not an end in itself.

6. *Credible.* Measures should be objective and applied consistently throughout of the organization. The measurement and its calculation methodology should be well-defined and well-documented to minimize the possibility of manipulation by managers or employees. The absence of these characteristics can seriously undermine the credibility of a performance measurement system.

Two more attributes should be added to this list:

7. *Dynamic.* Performance measures will change over time as the business evolves, strategies change, and priorities shift. A periodic reassessment of these measures ensures that they remain up to date and still maintain their relevance for the organization.

8. *Forward-looking.* Performance measures should not only look at the past, but should alert management to potential problems in the future. They should provide early warning signals in critical areas so that management can take corrective actions or modify its plans accordingly.

Performance measures should emphasize the critical dimensions of performance that are vital to an organization's long-term success: quality, cost, customer service, time to market, and social responsibility. However, traditional performance measurement systems have focused on financial results, which only assess one dimension of performance and may overlook critical aspects such as quality or customer service that may seriously affect the economic viability of the organization in the future. These recognized weaknesses of performance measurement systems have pushed organizations to develop integrated performance management systems (I-PMS). I-PMS is viewed as an enterprise management system that links strategies, critical success factors, high-priority change initiatives, and key performance indicators in a coherent framework. It is a closed loop management system in which the implementation of strategy results in a learning process that is fed back into the planning cycle of the organization. These systems promote a more balanced view of the organization and emphasize the use of leading indicators, as well as nonfinancial quantitative and qualitative measures, to identify opportunities and problem areas that require action. Figure 8.1 shows the closed loop nature of an I-PMS and how it brings together planning, implementation, measurement, and evaluation under one management structure. It also shows how an I-PMS at a macro level fits into the PDCA framework (plan-do-check-act) developed by Dr. W. Edwards Deming, founder of the total quality management movement (TQM).[2]

One of the more widely known performance management models is the Balanced Scorecard, developed by Robert Kaplan and David Norton. The Balanced Scorecard provides a mechanism to translate strategies into tangible objectives and measures, which are then aligned throughout the

Figure 8.1 Integrated Performance Management Systems

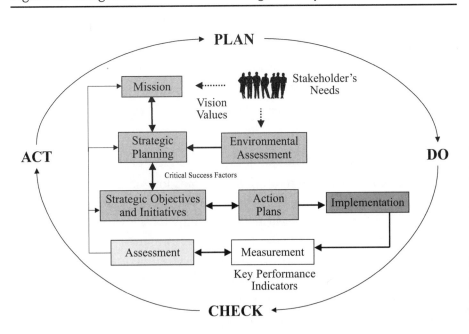

organization. It seeks to capture the value drivers of an organization by using an integrated set of performance measures to describe, communicate, and measure the strategy used for value creation. It views the business across four different perspectives—financial, customer, internal/business process, and learning and growth—and shows what must occur within each of these perspectives to attain the desired goals and to achieve long-term economic performance.[3]

Other lesser-known performance management models also emphasize a balanced approach to evaluating organizational execution. The Skandia Navigator is a proprietary performance measurement model, developed by Skandia Corporation, to manage intellectual capital, which Skandia defines as the unique combination of customers, employees, and processes that drive value creation.[4] Because Skandia operates a diversified financial services business, metrics are industry specific or business specific. For example, occupancy percentages are very important for the real estate business, but meaningless for the bank or insurance subsidiary. Skandia used the Navigator framework as the basis for its Intellectual Capital report from 1994 to 1998. The company continues to use the Navigator for internal reporting purposes and is currently reevaluating its approach to external disclosure of intellectual capital.

The Intangible Assets Monitor (IAM) is another performance management model developed by Swedish management consultant Karl-Erik Sveiby based on the concept of the knowledge organization. It provides a mechanism for measuring intangible assets and presenting a number of relevant indicators in a simple manner. The choice of indicators depends on the company strategy. The IAM divides intangible assets into three major categories:

1. *External structure indicators,* which look at customers, suppliers, and other external stakeholders

2. *Internal structure indicators,* which examine the activities and people who work in general management, accounting, information systems, and other internal support processes

3. *Competence indicators,* which look at the activities and people who are directly involved in client work

Within each category, a set of indicators is defined to report growth/ renewal, efficiency, and stability. Though the IAM model is designed for professional services or consulting firms, its underlying conceptual framework can be easily applied to other types of industries.[5]

Figure 8.2 shows a comparison of the Balanced Scorecard, the Skandia Navigator, and the IAM. All three models support the notion that a company's value is the sum of its tangible and intangible assets. The tangible assets represent the buildings, equipment, and general infrastructure that are currently measured by financial accounting systems. The intangible assets are the combination of customers, employees, and business processes, which use the tangible assets of the organization to create economic value. These are more difficult to identify and quantify in meaningful terms, but are at the crux of developing a balanced approach to managing the organization.

Each organization should determine their particular approach to performance measurement taking into consideration the management philosophy, the organizational culture, the purpose of the system, and the availability of information. However, managers should recognize the need to integrate strategy and performance measurement into a solid management structure that can be used to evaluate progress toward company goals. This structure should be based on a balanced set of measures to

Figure 8.2 Comparison of Performance Management Approaches

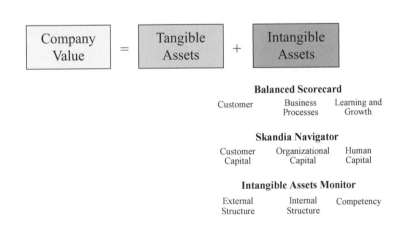

ensure that no single dimension of performance will take priority over other critical dimensions that may affect the organization's value creating potential.

WHERE DOES THE COST SYSTEM FIT IN?

Most performance measurement systems include some type of cost measure. Some popular cost metrics include unit costs, overtime, costs as percent of sales, and budget variances. Some cost measures will be readily available because they reside in your formal accounting systems such as standard costs and manufacturing variances. Other cost indicators such as excess capacity costs, unutilized labor costs, scrap, and rework may require agreement on how the measure will be calculated and reported.

Cost measures that are used for performance measurement and decision support should be consistent with the methodology and operational parameters that underlie the cost model of the organization. Line managers sometimes include cost information in their reports that has neither been reviewed nor validated by a finance representative. When this type of information is presented in a management meeting, the discussion often deteriorates into a "he-said, she-said" situation with line managers and cost analysts both pointing out the flaws in each other's numbers. The discussion revolves around how the numbers were calculated versus the business issues behind the numbers. Therefore, in a cost system redesign project, the team should identify what cost measures will be included as part of the key performance indicators and how this information will be collected and reported. An agreement upfront will allow managers to focus on the business issues going forward, rather than how the cost information was collected and calculated.

The cost system also can provide a vital link between the implementation of strategy and the financial results. As discussed in Chapter 6, the cost of providing products and services is based on a set of operational parameters that are driven by organizational strategy. These operational parameters relate to yield, process efficiency, labor productivity, capacity utilization, quality, and customer service.

Performance measurement systems typically integrate some or all of these operational parameters as key metrics in their management reporting although they are not necessarily linked to their financial implications. The ability to quantify these performance metrics in monetary terms is one of the most important value-adding functions of a good cost system. An example will illustrate this point. Suppose you are the production manager of a large pharmaceutical manufacturing subsidiary. Top management has established cost reduction as a key strategic objective, and you are trying to decide which product you should target for process improvement in the upcoming months. Product and average yield information for the last quarter is shown in Figure 8.3. Which product would you choose? Based on the information solely provided in Figure 8.3, you would probably choose Product C, which has the highest unfavorable yield variance. However, when you overlay costs on the yield information for these products, a different picture emerges, as shown in Figure 8.4. Based on this information, you would probably target Product B for process improvement, because even though it has the highest yield, it also has a high manufacturing cost. Therefore, a small improvement in yield could potentially have a large financial impact.

The cost system should also address those costs that may underlie key performance measures but are not captured in the company's *general ledger*.[6] Many decisions result in lost opportunities. When a production line or a service facility shuts down temporarily, there are costs incurred that are not adequately reflected in the financial statements. One is the cost of the labor, space, and equipment that remains unused for this time period; another is the lost revenue as a result of the shutdown. Traditional

Figure 8.3 Comparison of Actual versus Standard Manufacturing Yields

Product	Actual Yield*	Yield Variance
A	93%	(4%)
B	95%	(3%)
C	90%	(9%)

* **Actual yield** represents the actual output divided by the theoretical yield. Yield variance is the difference between the actual and the standard yield. For example, the standard yield for Product A is 97% versus the actual yield of 93%, resulting in an unfavorable yield variance of 4%.

Figure 8.4 Presentation of Yield Variance in Dollars

Product	Actual Yield	Yield Variance	Yield Variance in Dollars
A	93%	(4%)	$45,000
B	95%	(3%)	$60,000
C	90%	(9%)	$30,000

financial reports typically do not include these type of costs, although many times they are implicitly considered in the decision-making process of a manager. As part of the integration of the cost system with the performance measurement system, the team should identify those key performance measures that should be costed and should establish how these costs will be calculated. For example, a service or manufacturing facility, which is evaluated as a *cost center*, might decide to report downtime hours and show its impact on the financial results for the period based on the cost per process hour of running the line.[7] However, another facility, which is evaluated as a *profit center*, might decide to calculate the cost of downtime in terms of the lost revenue opportunities versus the cost of running the line.[8] The team should recognize that the costs of nonfinancial performance measures are an estimate of their true costs. The purpose of this costing exercise is to provide managers with a cost estimate to guide them in their day-to-day decision-making process. A 99 percent order fill rate has a different cost implication than a 95 percent order fill rate, both in terms of the resources required and the revenue gained or lost as a result of this execution. By tying the difference in performance level to costs, managers can understand the financial consequences of their decisions for the future. Figure 8.5 shows a sample of a management report that integrates the traditional budget-versus-actual report with the key performance measures for the business unit. This type of report would substitute the traditional departmental spending or responsibility report prepared by accountants at the end of a reporting period. Any financial report can be restructured using this approach. The key lies in identifying those critical performance indicators that overlay the operating environment on the financial information being reported.

Figure 8.5 Sample Performance Report

Production Department XYZ
For the Six-Month Period Ending MMYY

OPERATIONS SUMMARY	Actual	YTD Budget	Variance
Customer Service			
• Backlog (units)	159,455	–	159,455
• Backlog (in dollars)	$478,365	–	$478,365
Production			
Production (units)	1,600,000	1,750,000	−150,000
Schedule attainment	90%	100%	0
Labor utilization	75%	80%	0
Process efficiency	82.29%	90.00%	0
Cost improvement opportunity	$354,992	–	$354,992
Labor Productivity			
Units produced per employee	38,095	38,889	−794
Financial			
Average cost per unit	$2.21	$1.99	$0.22
Work in process inventory	$176,256	$86,927	$ 89,329

COST SUMMARY	YTD Actual	YTD Budget	Variance
Direct materials	$1,630,000	$1,488,387	$141,613
Water	141,00	5125,338	15,667
Electricity	119,521	78,336	41,185
Subtotal variable costs	**$1,890,526**	**$1,692,061**	**$198,465**
Labor	673,691	735,000	−61,309
Depreciation	391,681	437,500	−45,819
Maintenance and repairs	156,672	192,500	−35,828
Insurance	15,667	5,250	10,417
Professional services	7,834	3,500	4,334
Other	6,267	–	6,267
Subtotal fixed costs	**$1,251,812**	**$1,373,750**	**($121,938)**
Total controllable costs	**$3,142,338**	**$3,065,811**	**$ 76,527**
Support services from other areas	391,681	411,250	(19,569)
Total departmental costs	**$3,534,019**	**$3,477,061**	**$ 56,958**

When dollars are tied to nonfinancial indicators and these are significant, it will definitely catch management's attention. During a management meeting of one of my clients, the quality manager presented the scrap figures for the prior fiscal year in pounds and dollars. The owner of the business was floored by the numbers. Although the organization had been reporting scrap on a regular basis, it was the first time he had seen dollars attached to the scrap figures. He immediately created a task force to work on reducing scrap in the facility.

Not all operational parameters in your cost system will form part of the key performance metrics in the organization. For example, if an organization requires a fixed level of employees to run a particular process regardless of customer demand, labor utilization might not be a meaningful measure for its line managers. In addition, although nonfinancial performance measures can usually be quantified in financial terms, the organization may choose to continue reporting only the nonfinancial indicator because the cost implications are well understood by its managers.

In sum, the cost system needs to be integrated with the performance measurement system of the organization. In this manner, management can ensure that cost information is presented and reported in a manner that is consistent with the formal accounting systems and can be tied to the financial results.

MANAGEMENT REPORTING

Performance measurement and management reporting go hand in hand. Management reporting provides the mechanism to ensure that relevant information is communicated in a timely manner to affect the decision-making process. Because the format and presentation of the information can enhance or detract from its effectiveness as a decision support tool, any cost system redesign project must pay particularly close attention to how cost information will be accessed and disseminated throughout the organization.

The cost system will provide the basis for preparing both financial and operational reports. Operational reports measure how well the organization has performed against a standard or targeted goal. Typically, they report on output, yield, efficiency, asset utilization, product or service quality, scrap levels, overtime, absenteeism, asset turnover, and many other operational parameters that drive a company's costs. In my experience, many of these operational reports already exist and are being used by the line managers. The key, however, is linking the information contained in these reports to show their impact on financial performance.

Financial reports can take on many different formats and are usually limited to reporting financial information. Although more forward-thinking organizations have started to incorporate key performance indicators as part of their internal (and sometimes external) reporting process, their use for this purpose has yet to gain widespread acceptance among the accounting profession. The AICPA and other accounting organizations have conducted several studies on financial reporting, which discuss the importance of nonfinancial indicators and their potential integration into a business reporting model.[9] Although the accounting profession has made no definitive pronouncement on this issue, the dissatisfaction with the current financial reporting model seems to indicate that we will see an increase in the use of non-financial indicators in internal and external financial reports in the future.

As the project team evaluates the management reports available in the organization, they should consider the following questions:

- What financial and operational reports are currently produced in the organization? With what frequency? How will the new cost system affect the way information is presented in these reports?
- What is the purpose of these reports? Who uses them?
- Do they contain information that is actionable by line management?
- Does the information presented in these reports further the company's strategic objectives?
- Is the information easy to understand and use? Is the format understandable to its primary users?
- Is there a way to link financial and operational data to provide a more meaningful representation of the business? Is there any supplemental information that management would like to have reported?

The team should also focus on the level of management that will be reviewing the report. As the information moves up the organizational hierarchy, it should be more summarized and provide the user with drill-down capabilities to obtain additional information as required. For example, an engineer in manufacturing or service operations who is monitoring equipment reliability will probably require a different level of detail in her reports than the business unit manager, who may want a more summarized view of this aspect of the operations.

VARIANCE REPORTING

Variance analysis has traditionally been the accountant's tool to analyze differences between actual costs and expected financial results. For companies that use a standard cost system, variance analysis lies at the heart of this system and accountants spend a significant amount of hours analyzing the variances to the standard cost. Unfortunately, this analysis often fails to have a significant impact on the day-to-day business decisions. Nonfinancial managers complain that they are asked to explain variances that arise from changes in business conditions that are well known to management. Another frequent complaint is that information presented is too summarized or in a format that is difficult to understand and use.

Variance analysis should highlight opportunities for cost reduction and continuous improvement. As part of the cost system redesign, the accounting representatives on the team should take a hard look at their variance reporting system. Is variance reporting designed to be a decision support tool or is it mostly for use by the accountants? Does it address the needs of its audience? Is the design of the report intimidating to a nonfinancial user? Can a nonfinancial user understand, analyze, and act on the information contained in the report? Since by this stage of the redesign process the team will have agreed on the operational parameters driving the costs, variance reporting should focus on deviations from these parameters and their financial consequences. A well-designed report can highlight opportunities for action, but line managers must identify the causal factors that create a variation from the expected results and act on the information. Here is where the cost system, performance measurement, and management reporting converge to create an integrated performance management system.

SUMMARY

In Chapter 1, we discussed performance measurement and decision support as two important functions of an effective cost system. A cost system that only calculates and reports total and unit costs will not significantly affect how the business is run because it is not integrated with the key performance measures that are being used to manage the company. However, integration with the performance measurement system is not sufficient to guarantee that cost information will have an effect on management or employees' behavior. The information should be communicated in a way that is simple, easy to understand, and actionable by the user. It can be demotivating to managers and employees to be held accountable for metrics that they cannot significantly influence. In my experience, many cost systems do not function effectively as a decision support tool because they are not integrated into the performance measurement system of the organization. In addition, financial information is poorly presented and explained to nonfinancial managers. The project team should explicitly address these two issues as part of the overall system redesign in order to build an effective cost system that will endure the test of time.

ENDNOTES

1. See "Developing Comprehensive Performance Indicators," Statements on Management Accounting 4U (May 31, 1995), 24–25.

2. For more information on the total quality management philosophy, see Dr. W. Edwards Deming, *Out of the Crisis* (Boston: MIT Press, 2000).

3. For more information on the Balance Scorecard, see Robert S. Kaplan and David P. Norton, "The Balanced Scorecard—Measures that Drive Performance," *Harvard Business Review* (January–February 1992); and Robert S. Kaplan and David P. Norton, "Putting the Balanced Scorecard to Work," *Harvard Business Review* (September–October 1993). A more comprehensive explanation of the Balance Scorecard can be found in Robert S. Kaplan and David P. Norton, *The Balance Scorecard:*

Translating Strategy Into Action (Boston: Harvard Business School Publishing, 1996), and Robert S. Kaplan and David P. Norton, *The Strategy-Focused Organization: How Balance Scorecard Companies Thrive in the New Business Environment* (Boston: Harvard Business School Publishing, 2001).

4. For more information, see *www.skandia.com.*

5. For more information on the Intangible Assets Monitor (IAM), see *www.sveiby.com.* For a real-world application of the Intangible Assets Monitor, see the 2002 Annual Report of Celemi, available at *www.celemi.com,* under the section titled "About Celemi— Organization."

6. The *general ledger* is the database that contains a record of all the financial transactions of the company. Financial transactions are recorded, summarized, and reported by accounts, which are classifications determined by management to organize the information in a meaningful manner.

7. *Cost centers* are units whose managers are only accountable for costs; a cost center manager typically controls the inputs to the process (e.g., manpower and materials), but has no control over sales or the generation of revenue.

8. *Profit centers* are evaluated based on the operating income or net income of the particular subunits of the organization. Ideally, a profit center manager should influence all major factors affecting revenues and costs such as pricing, sales and marketing strategies, and sources of supply.

9. For more information, see Wayne S. Upton Jr., "Business and Financial Reporting, Challenges from the New Economy," *Financial Accounting Series Special Report No. 219A* (Norwalk, CT: Financial Accounting Standards Board, April 2001).

9

Common Pitfalls

Some cost redesign projects die before they reach the implementation stage. Others are successfully implemented but fall into obsolescence with the passage of time. There are many reasons why cost redesign projects fail to achieved their original objectives. Some reasons are beyond the control of the organization, but more often, they fail because of a lack of commitment, inadequate resources, unrealistic timeframes, or a combination of all of the above. In this chapter, we will explore the common pitfalls that can undermine a cost redesign project and lead to its eventual demise. We will also discuss some proactive steps that you can take to ensure your redesigned cost system is successfully implemented and withstands the test of time.

PITFALLS

The following situations are common pitfalls that may hinder a project's chances of success. By acknowledging and addressing these issues up front, the team can increase the likelihood of achieving its desired goals.

Accounting Versus Operations-Driven Projects

In my experience, a project that is initiated and driven by accountants has a much lower chance of success than one that is set up at the request of line management. Accountants generally lack the depth of technical know-how to identify the key operational parameters that are driving costs. The knowledge and cooperation of line managers is essential in order to design a cost system that reflects the reality of the business processes. Because the project will consume a significant amount of time, line managers must understand up front the benefits that they will reap from the new cost system. If they perceive the project as another accounting proposal, they may be reluctant to commit resources and even sabotage any change initiative. My most successful cost redesign projects have been initiated at the request of line managers who felt a growing dissatisfaction with the cost information supplied by their accountants.

Top Management Is Not Committed

The top management of an organization needs to be committed to the project and reflect this commitment in terms of the organizational priorities and resources. Cost redesign projects are expensive undertakings. They usually involve a team of highly paid professionals from different functional areas and may sometimes require the intervention of an outside consultant. In addition, there may be other costs such as temporary labor, seminars, training materials, and the purchase of hardware, software, or both. Top management must be willing to provide the project with the necessary funding to achieve its objectives within the expected timeframe.

They must also be willing to shift organizational priorities to meet project milestones. The day-to-day operations often threaten to overwhelm individual team members, causing them to miss deadlines and affecting the performance of the entire project team. When this situation happens, top management can reassign priorities or shift responsibilities to other individuals in the organization so that team members can focus on completing their assigned tasks. If top management is not committed, this reprioritization does not take place and the project deadlines continue to slip. Eventually, the project comes to a screeching halt and is replaced with other projects and initiatives. If team members do not perceive a true commitment from top management, they should not move forward with the project. It is a waste of time and resources to initiate a project that does not have the full support of top management.

Lack of Resources

In the era of continuous improvement, organizations are continually asking their managers to do more with less. In some organizations, individuals are asked to participate in the project team, but are not relieved from their day-to-day responsibilities. This situation results in missed deadlines, incomplete or unfinished tasks, and project delays. If a person already has a full-time job, it is not realistic to expect the person to continue performing these responsibilities at the same level and participate in a project of this magnitude. Something has got to give. If top management is committed, usually an alternative is found to the possible lack of resources for the project—whether it is people, space, or equipment. If not, they will probably ask the team to make do with whatever resources are available in the organization. A word of caution—when the lack of resources threatens to affect the completion of a project milestone, the team members are responsible for raising the red flag to top management. Top management can then decide how important this project really is in light of other organizational priorities.

Unrealistic Timeframes

This difficulty seems the plague of corporate America—we want it all done yesterday. Team members, in their enthusiasm for the project, often set unreasonable expectations and commit to dates that are not realistic in light of their other responsibilities. Because some tasks involved in a redesign project are sequential in nature, if one team member fails to deliver, it will have a domino effect on the entire project schedule. For example, if the industrial engineer fails to supply time standards, the accountant will not have the operational data required to develop product or service costs.

In my experience, a cost redesign project can take anywhere from six months to two years, depending on the resources devoted to the project. An aggressive implementation schedule will require a greater commitment of resources to get the job completed on time. Team members should evaluate if they have the resources to complete the project within the expected timeframe or if management expectations need to be adjusted based on the resources that have been assigned to the project.

Established Systems or Procedures

A corporation may have an established policy or procedure on how to develop costs. These policies and procedures may limit the range of options for the new system design. The team cannot start from a blank slate, but must develop costs and provide information within the established corporate framework. Multinational corporations, for example, usually issue some type of guidelines to ensure consistency and comparability of cost information across sites. If the team designs a system that is radically different from the corporate framework, it is highly unlikely that they will be allowed to implement this design.

Information systems applications can also provide roadblocks to the implementation of the cost system design. Software applications may not have the capabilities to develop and report costs as envisioned by the team. In this situation, the team might have to develop a workaround solution or compromise the design to accommodate the systems limitations. It is important to document these workarounds or compromises to the system design. If the system restrictions are eliminated through a software upgrade or the purchase of a new application, the cost system setup can be revisited in light of the new capabilities of the system.

Lack of Expertise

Sometimes, team members lack the accounting or operational expertise to form part of the project team. This situation can significantly hinder the progress of the project. As discussed in Chapter 3, the project team should consist of the best and the brightest individuals in the organization. They should be functional experts who understand the interrelationships and dependencies with the other areas that are represented on the team. When this expertise is lacking in a particular team member, tasks are not completed in a satisfactory manner and the whole team effort is affected by the situation. It often results in delays or rework, as other team members must pick up the slack for the individual in question. Perhaps the most difficult situation to manage is when the team member does not recognize that he does not have the expertise and continues to make commitments and promises that he cannot keep. If the team is confronted with this situation, I recommend raising the red flag immediately to the next level of management and finding an appropriate substitute for the problem performer. If not, the success of the project will be jeopardized.

Staff Turnover

Individuals constantly enter and leave an organization. However, when this individual is the project manager or the project champion, it can signal the death knell of a cost redesign project.

I have personally been involved in two cost redesign projects where a key player left in the middle of the implementation. In one organization, it killed the project. Although changes were made to the costing methodology, once the cost standards were finalized, the organizational priorities shifted and with the project champion gone, there was no one left in the organization to push the project forward to completion. In another organization, a new project manager was recruited who continued the cost redesign effort. Although the project was delayed for about six months, the organization was able to bring the project to fruition.

So what happens when there is a sudden change in management? I was involved in a project where both the plant manager and the controller of a manufacturing site were replaced rather suddenly. However, the project had the support of corporate headquarters and had been identified as a top priority for this site. When the new management came on board, they were briefed on the cost project and its importance—not only for the site, but also as a pilot project for the corporation. The controller met with me, as the project facilitator, and then with the project team to discuss our objectives, deliverables, progress to date, and deadlines. He became our most staunch supporter.

Lack of Information Systems Support

Information systems must be part of the project team from the start. Inevitably, the project team will face the issue of how to set up the cost system within the context of the current information systems applications. If information systems personnel are not available to assist the project team in this endeavor, it could become a critical roadblock for the project.

Enterprise management systems are complex, highly integrated applications. Typically there is no one person in the organization that understands the full functionality of the system and how the different modules interact with one another. The information systems specialist assigned to the team should have relevant expertise in the applications that will be affected by the team decisions or be able to identify internal or external resources that can provide this expertise to the team.

Mergers, Acquisitions, and Reorganizations

A merger, acquisition, or any type of organizational restructuring will probably bring the project to a temporary halt. It will require the team to revalidate its objectives, deliverables, and deadlines with the new management before continuing to move forward. It will probably delay the implementation timetable as the organization settles under the new administrative structure. However, a significant organizational restructuring can also result in the demise of the project as the new management shifts priorities to other areas.

Recognition of the Potential Pitfalls

When embarking on a cost system redesign project, team members should recognize the difficulties that they may face during this process and seek ways to minimize their impact on the attainment of the project goals. Some obstacles that will be encountered, such as mergers and reorganizations, are beyond the control of the team or, often, of the company management. Others, however, can be averted by addressing these issues upfront during the initial project organization. The team should incorporate sufficient flexibility into its process to accommodate any unforeseen events that might have a bearing on the project.

WITHSTANDING THE TEST OF TIME

A cost system redesign project ends when all project deliverables have been accomplished. The deliverables are usually completed in stages, starting with the development of product or service costs and ending with the identification of key performance measures and the design of management reports. When the project is completed, the team should formally close the project by presenting the final results to top management, highlighting any open actions that will require follow-up.

Organizations are dynamic entities that evolve with the passage of time. The inability to maintain the cost system updated with the latest information on the business processes is one of the primary reasons that cost systems fall into obsolescence and disuse. Performance measures and reports should also be periodically reexamined to ensure that the information presented is still relevant and useful to management. If there has been a dramatic change in the business, even the costing methodology might need to be revisited.

The project team can take four steps prior to project closure that will increase the longevity of the new cost system once the team has disbanded:

1. *Ensure that all aspects of the system are documented.* The preparation of a cost manual is critical to ensure the transfer of knowledge to other individuals in the organization. It provides a key training vehicle for employees as individuals change jobs or enter and exit the organization. The documentation should describe the methods used to set time standards and explain how to calculate products or service costs. Key performance measures should be defined, and their relevance to management decision making should be documented. Sample reports should also be included in the documentation.

2. *Train users.* Training is a critical aspect of the implementation process. It ensures that there is a transfer of knowledge from the team to other members of the organization. The training can be done in a formal seminar setting or on a one-to-one basis. It should cover the conceptual framework of the system, changes to operational and accounting procedures, and management reports. Each cross-functional area responsible for a specific aspect of the cost system should ensure that its key users are trained so that critical information required to calculate or report costs does not reside in any one individual.

3. *Clearly identify areas of responsibility.* The team should assign specific areas of responsibility to particular groups or individuals in the organization. There should be no gray areas in terms of who is responsible for providing information that feeds the cost system. For example, industrial engineering or production management is typically responsible for reviewing and updating information on yield, time standards, and operational performance measures,

while finance handles the calculation of unit costs and tying key operational parameters to their cost implications.

4. *Establish a formal review of the cost system at least once a year.* The team should establish a formal process for reviewing and updating the system at least once a year. This review should occur during the budgeting process unless there is a major upheaval to the business processes or the organizational structure that warrants an immediate evaluation of the cost system.

But perhaps the most important step the team can take is to maintain open the lines of communication across functional areas so that future business issues that affect costs or the design of the cost system can be managed from a systemic perspective.

SUMMARY

The redesign of a new cost system will be faced with many challenges. These will either be overcome by the project team or will lead to the project's demise. In this chapter, we have discussed common pitfalls that can threaten the successful completion of a cost system redesign project. Some can be managed by the organization, and others will be beyond its control. The key is management commitment. If top management is committed and line managers support the project, resources will usually be found and obstacles will be removed. A strong commitment from top management greatly increases the likelihood of a successful project implementation.

10

Lessons Learned

The redesign of a cost system is a major organizational undertaking. A successful redesign requires a clear definition of purpose, specific project deliverables, and cross-functional involvement. It also requires an understanding of the six major elements of a cost system and how these interact to provide financial and decision support information for its management. A focus on one or several elements is not enough. A robust cost system requires attention to all six elements.

Throughout this book, I have threaded several major themes that highlight important issues that should be addressed as part of a cost redesign project. This chapter summarizes these major themes to ensure that they are considered at each stage of the project. These themes represent lessons learned from my consulting practice in this area, which are strongly supported by the accounting literature on the subject. Attention to these issues up front greatly increases the chances of a successful project implementation.

MANAGEMENT MUST BE COMMITTED

We discussed this issue at length in the prior chapter. *Top management commitment significantly increases the likelihood of a successful outcome.* Lack of top management commitment will usually result in a waste of time and resources as the project is overwhelmed by the day-to-day priorities of the organization.

Actions, however, speak louder than words. If top management verbally expresses its commitment, but continually refuses to shift priorities to achieve a project milestone, it is sending a clear message of the importance of the cost redesign project to the organization. Commitment means resources, and resources mean money. Top management must express its commitment not only by allocating resources and funds to the project, but also by changing or shifting priorities to get the job done.

PROJECT TEAM MUST BE COMMITTED

The project team should consist of individuals who are highly motivated and who have technical expertise in their area of responsibility. You want the best and the brightest on the project team and should avoid the assignment of mediocre or problem performers. Remember, the team is only as strong as its weakest link. A poor performer can drag down the performance of the entire team, particularly if they are responsible for a critical task. Ideally, team members should consist of technical experts who are highly regarded in the organization and can add credibility to the project through their participation.

SET A REALISTIC PROJECT SCHEDULE

In their enthusiasm to get the job done, individual team members or the team as a whole tend to commit to timeframes that are unrealistic in light of their current job responsibilities. Team members should consider events such as budgeting, board presentations, quarter or year-end reporting, physical inventory, and any other major organizational event when planning the project schedule. In addition, they should incorporate some type of contingency planning to allow for the unexpected. There will always be some last-minute request or business situation that may hinder that team's ability to meet an aggressive implementation deadline. By incorporating some cushion into the project schedule, team members can handle unforeseen events without affecting their ability to complete project milestones.

KNOW YOUR LIMITATIONS AND CONSTRAINTS

You do not want to design a system that cannot be implemented due to corporate policy or system constraints. The team should understand these limitations and constraints up front and design the system accordingly.

One common limitation in multinational corporations is the type of costs that can be used. For example, if your company operates under a standard cost system, it is highly unlikely that you will be allowed to implement a system using actual costs. Another area is in the classification of fixed, variable, and semivariable costs. Corporate policy may define certain categories of expense as fixed or variable, when the operational reality is just the opposite. For example, in some pharmaceutical manufacturers, direct labor is not a variable cost because certain operations require a minimum number of employees, regardless of the volume produced during any particular shift. However, the corporate accounting policy requires the classification of these costs as variable.

In addition to policy constraints, the team may face information system constraints. These limitations can become showstoppers or significantly affect the system design. My experience is that many software applications use a very traditional approach in collecting data from the business operations and calculating product or service costs. If the team wants to use a nontraditional costing approach or wants to gather data on a specific operational parameter, it may require a systems workaround or the development of a subroutine outside the formal systems application to collect or manipulate the data.

The environmental, policy, or systems constraints can affect the scope, design, or implementation plan of the project. Although a team might decide to break a systems constraint or propose a change to management policy, the identification of these limitations early on in the design process is important so that the team can develop its work plan accordingly. It will also reduce the likelihood of completing a system design that cannot be implemented given the current management philosophy, corporate structure, or information systems.

DO WHAT MAKES SENSE FOR THE BUSINESS

Every organization is a unique entity with its particular culture, organizational structure, level of maturity, systems, and people. All these factors should be considered in the cost system design for an organization. Two firms in the same industry may have radically different cost systems that meet the business needs equally well because of the uniqueness of their operating environment. The latest and greatest management theory or costing approach is not always the best solution for an organization. I call my cost systems design approach *simple elegance*. The goal is to design and implement a system that will meet the needs of the organization in the simplest and most cost-effective manner possible. It may involve the use of advanced management or costing techniques such as activity-based costing, balanced scorecard, target costing, or throughput accounting. It may incorporate Monte Carlo simulations and sophisticated statistical analyses in defining or determining the parameters that drive costs. However, it may consist of a traditional standard cost system that allocates overhead based on direct labor hours and uses traditional financial performance measures to report results. For example, an organization in which materials represents 90 to 95 percent of total product costs may find little value in the implementation of an ABC methodology, but may find great value in performing an activity analysis of its major business processes.

Sometimes external consultants try to impose their particular approach or management philosophy upon the project team without considering what makes sense for the organization. While the project team should be exposed to a broad range of possible options in developing the conceptual framework of their cost system, it should mix and match to find the right set of tools that will produce accurate costs and provide performance measures for evaluation and decision support appropriate for the organization and its business environment.

KEEP MANAGEMENT INFORMED

Make sure your key managers are kept abreast of the team's progress and enlist their support in any key decisions made by the project team. Copy all key players on the minutes of the team meetings and, when necessary, invite them to participate in discussions of particular issues that may affect their area. Have checkpoint meetings with top management after the completion of a major project milestone. Checkpoint meetings are important forums to receive feedback from top management and obtain their buy-in. However, they are not the time or place to air out controversies among different organizational units. Potential conflicts and differences of opinion should be identified and discussed prior to a checkpoint meeting.

KEEP YOUR COST SYSTEM CURRENT

An organization is a dynamic entity that will evolve and change with the passage of time. The cost system, as a reflection of operational processes, must also change and evolve with the organization or risk falling into functional obsolescence. Although it might still calculate and report costs, these costs will not reflect current business conditions and will be useless as a performance measurement and decision support tool. If your cost system is to withstand the test of time, the project team must provide a mechanism to review all six elements of the costing methodology on a periodic basis, but no less than once a year. If your business is fairly stable, you should not see any major changes over time. However, if you have undergone any type of organizational restructuring, have obtained new clients, transferred products, or implemented a new technology, there may be some significant changes to the original cost system design.

In my experience, the operational parameters are usually the first element of a cost system that becomes obsolete. Line managers, pressed for time, do not review these drivers in light of the current operating environment and often take the prior year's numbers as valid. The lack of a systematic review of your operational parameters on a yearly basis is the first symptom that your cost system may be falling into obsolescence. Other areas that should be examined are the reporting formats and performance measures. Are they still valid, considering the changes to the business? Should reports or metrics be deleted? Should others be added? My recommendation is to perform a review of the cost system prior to the start of the annual budgeting process. This review will ensure that your costs reflect the current business conditions and are properly captured in the budget. If you are part of an organization that works on a rolling budget, you will need to determine at which point in the year a review of the cost system would produce the most benefit.

SUMMARY

Management should view a cost system redesign project as an investment in the intellectual and human capital of the organization. It presents a unique opportunity to examine the business processes of the organization from a systemic perspective and to identify opportunities for improvement.

It also provides an invaluable learning experience for team members, who develop a greater awareness of the interdependencies of the different functional areas and a heightened sensitivity on how their actions can affect the financial performance of the organization.

A strategic cost system should accurately reflect the business processes and meet the needs of its users in a timely and relevant manner. It should provide better information for management decision making and trigger changes to organizational disciplines and employee behavior that eventually lead to lower costs, higher quality, and improved customer service. However, a cost system, in and of itself, will not reduce costs or improve financial performance. It is the people behind the system that will determine its effectiveness as a financial and decision support tool. Information is power—but only to the extent that it is acted upon to achieve results.

In this book, I have presented a blueprint for the design and implementation of a strategic cost system. Each organization will face unique issues and challenges in designing a cost system to meet the needs of the organization. The following anecdote illustrates this point:[1]

> A wise man of ancient China was noted for his wisdom and ability to solve problems. One day a merchant came to him seeking advice. It seems that the merchant had a problem in his accounting department.
>
> "I have six men and six abacuses, but my needs have expanded to the point where I need a 20 percent increase in output. I cannot afford the capital investment of another man and another abacus; and even if I could, one man would not be enough, and two men would be too much."
>
> The wise man pondered the problem for several days and finally summoned the merchant.
>
> "The solution to your problem," he told him, "is simple. Each of your present accounting staff must grow another finger on each hand. This will increase your abacus output exactly 20 percent and solve your problem."
>
> The merchant smiled. His problem was solved. He started to leave, paused a moment, and looked at the wise old man. "Oh, Wise

One," he said, "you have truly given me the solution to my problem. But...," and he paused, "how do I get my people to grow extra fingers?"

The wise man puffed on his pipe. "That is a good question," he said. "But alas, I only make policy recommendations. The details of execution are up to you."

The transition from design to execution will determine effectiveness of the system to influence behavior and achieve results. Only a system that is workable for its users can unleash the power of cost information to improve the long-term economic performance of the organization.

ENDNOTE

1. Reprinted from *How To Be The Life of the Podium.* Copyright © 1991 Sylvia Simmons. Reprinted by permission of AMACOM, a division of American Management Association International, New York, NY. All rights reserved. *http://amanet.org.*

Appendix A

Examples of Terms and Definitions

The following terms and definitions are examples that can be used as a boilerplate to develop cost terminology that is unique for your organization. You may copy these definitions to a word processing program and modify them to reflect the business processes of your company. Words placed in brackets [ ] represent alternative choices, which have different costing implications.

These definitions are also available in a file named "Cost_Terms.doc" at *www.wiley.com/go/costsystems* (see "About the Web Site" in the front section of this book).

Standard costs are the sum of the standard labor, materials, and overhead costs required to produce a product or provide a service using the process specifications under [normal, efficient] operating conditions. These specifications are determined during the annual budgeting process. Overheads costs will [include, exclude] allocated charges from support departments such as facilities, engineering, and maintenance and [include, exclude] the general and administrative costs associated with running the site such as accounting, human resources, and information systems.

Expected costs are the sum of the labor, materials, and overhead costs using the most current process specifications as defined by line management. They differ from standard costs in that they reflect changes to the time or materials standards that occurred after the standard costs were finalized. Typically expected costs are based on the most current operational parameters, which are costed at standard rates.

Actual costs represent an approximation of the actual resources consumed to manufacture a product or provide a service. Actual materials costs are based on the actual materials consumed and the average actual cost of each materials component. Labor and overhead are applied to the product using a standard rate that is calculated based on the actual costs of the prior [three, six, nine, twelve] months.

Theoretical yield represents the maximum good output for a particular process based on the input of a key ingredient, component, or document and given the current process design and specifications.

Standard yield represents expected good output for a particular process under [normal, efficient] operating conditions and given the current process specifications. The difference between 100 percent and the standard yield represents the output that is lost as part of the normal process. This expected loss is included in the product cost.

Standard materials are the components, ingredients, supplies, or packaging components required to produce the expected output at each stage of the manufacturing or service delivery process. It takes into consideration the expected yield and scrap losses that will occur as a normal part of the process.

Scrap represents unusable materials or production units (whether partially or fully completed) that do not meet customer requirements.[1] These materials or units must either be sold at a minimal value or disposed of in a safe and reasonable manner.

  Normal scrap is inherent to the production process and arises even under the efficient operating conditions. It should be included in the product cost based on the units of good output.

  Abnormal scrap is defective materials or units of output that are not inherent to the process and should not occur under efficient operating conditions, such as defects caused by a power outage or a lack of employee training. This type of scrap will be charged to cost of sales as a loss in the period incurred.

The scrap factor quantifies the amount of normal scrap that will be generated by the production process. It is expressed as a percentage of the quantity required for each component or ingredient and will be used to calculate the standard materials quantity for each item in the bill of materials.[2]

Rework represents units of production that do not meet customer specifications and are subsequently repaired. Rework costs are considered a loss in the period incurred and expensed to cost of sales.

Standard run time is the labor or machine time consumed in manufacturing the product or providing the service. It is based on the current process specifications under [normal, efficient] operating conditions. Standard time will include a provision for *unavoidable operator allowances* and *unavoidable delays.*

Normal operating conditions describe the environment in which a product is manufactured or the service delivery process takes place. It should consider the common allowances and delays that occur during the process. Normal operating conditions are usually determined based on historical experience.

Unavoidable operator allowance includes a provision for operator fatigue and any other unscheduled breaks that might affect labor productivity. This allowance is factored into the standard for the particular operation and should be excluded from the planned allowances that are included in the *total labor hours available per employee* calculation.

Unavoidable delays includes a provision for unscheduled interruptions such as equipment reliability and any other factors that may affect the production or service delivery process. This allowance is factored into the standard for the particular operation.

Setup includes all activities performed at the start and end of a business process such as equipment setup, material handling, assembly, disassembly, documentation, and cleanup. The activities that occur at the start of an operation will be measured separately from the activities performed at the end of an operation to identify potential process improvements.

Process time is the time required to complete a particular operation. It is the sum of the setup time plus the standard run time. Process time does not include queue time or the waiting time between operations.

Theoretical capacity will be based on 3 eight-hour shifts, 7 days per week, 52 weeks per year.[3]

Practical capacity will be based on 2 eight-hour shifts, 5 days per week, 48 weeks per year.

Available capacity is calculated based on the number of manned shifts for a particular time period.

Total labor hours available per employee represent the productive time available per employee after subtracting planned allowances for nonproductive time. It is calculated by taking labor hours paid based on a 2,080-hour year (40 hours per week x 52 weeks) less planned allowances such as holidays, vacations, sick leave, breaks, and others. Nonproductive time related to management decisions such as training or meetings will be included in the planned allowances and deducted from the total labor hours available per employee. Nonproductive time due to requirements of the process such as uniform changes or showering may be included in the time standards.

Actual hours used are the actual process or labor hours that were used to produce the actual output for the period.

ENDNOTES

1. In management accounting theory, scrap is called *spoilage*, which is defined as unacceptable units of production, whether fully or partially completed, that are discarded or sold for reduced value. In practice, however, managers use the term *scrap* for any type of defective material or product that does not meet customer specifications.

2. For simplicity, some companies use one scrap factor for all its components. If the scrap varies significantly from one type of materials to another, this decision may distort the true cost of the item under evaluation.

3. Capacity definitions should reflect the operating reality of your organization. These definitions provided are for illustration purposes only.

Appendix B

Time-Based Capacity Models

Time-based capacity models allow managers to establish the critical link between capacity utilization and costs in a relatively straightforward manner. They present information on capacity management and its impact on organizational performance. This appendix will provide a brief overview of two types of capacity reporting models: resource effectiveness models, which have traditionally been used by industrial engineers to analyze machine utilization, and the CAM-I Capacity Reporting Model. The detailed templates that support the examples discussed in this section are available in a file named "Appendix_B.Templates.xls" at *www.wiley.com/go/ costsystems* (see "About the Web Site" in the front section of this book).

RESOURCE EFFECTIVENESS REPORTING MODELS

Resource Effectiveness Reporting Models (RER) study the utilization of machinery and equipment in the business as a whole, in a department or work area, or by machine in the case of dedicated lines or expensive equipment. Although these models are based on industrial engineering concepts that focus primarily on machine utilization, their framework can be applied to analyze labor utilization as well.

RER models classify capacity utilization into several categories that show how capacity was used during a period and provide a series of effectiveness and efficiency ratios, which can be used to evaluate organizational performance. The goal is zero waste. The elements that will be included in each category of usage should be clearly defined by management. Although the specific elements may vary from company to company, they typically include the following categories:[1]

○ *Maximum time* represents the maximum possible time the process is available for production or service (e.g., 24 hours per day or 168 hours per week) within a given period. For a specific time horizon, the maximum time can be defined as theoretical capacity (24 hours per day, 365 days per year) or practical capacity, which would generally exclude holidays and other time off mandated by company or government policy. Many managers prefer to use practical capacity as the maximum available time, because it presents a more realistic view of the business.

○ *Available time* represents the time the facility or equipment could work based on manned shifts (the number of shifts running plus overtime hours). It is the equivalent of available capacity.

○ *Idle time* consists of all hours in which the equipment or facility is available for work, but are not being used due to market demand, materials shortages, or some other factor. Idle time represents unused or excess capacity, because although these hours are manned and ready for use, they are not employed in any manner whatsoever. It typically is caused by changes in market demand or variability in the production schedule, which results in short-term idle resources. This idleness is pure waste, since the costs associated with these idle resources will never be recovered through sales.

○ *Ancillary time* is the time involved in performing key support activities that are an integral part of the process, such as setup, cleanup, and changeovers.[2] The goal is to minimize the time spent in support activities so that this time can be used for productive purposes.

○ *Downtime* represents the time during which a process cannot be run, either for production or ancillary work due to an interruption in the work schedule. This interruption can be *planned* such as preventive maintenance, employee training, or communication meetings, or *unplanned* such as equipment breakdowns, labor or material shortages, and power outages, among others. The focus of a continuous improvement program should be on minimizing unplanned downtime, which can wreak havoc on your ability to meet customer requirements. Planned downtime should become a focus only if it is excessive in relation to the total productive time available.

○ *Run time* is the time the process is actually running. It is the available time less any downtime, idle time, or ancillary time. Run time should be subdivided into two categories: standard run time and run time losses. *Standard run time* is the standard time allowed for the volume produced or the services delivered. It is the amount of time that the organization should have taken to produce the product or service if the processes had run in an efficient manner. *Run time losses* are the loss of available hours as a result of process inefficiencies such as running an automated line at a slower pace than the standard rate.

RER models also provide a set of effectiveness and efficiency ratios, which can be used to evaluate how well capacity was used during the period and set stretch targets for future periods. Three ratios are commonly used. The *utilization index* measures the proportion of total hours the asset was utilized for productive purposes in relation to the total available time. It can provide an early warning signal to top management of an under or over utilization of capacity in a particular operation or facility. It is calculated by the dividing run time into available time. The *efficiency index* shows how close the asset operated to its optimal level. It is calculated by dividing the standard run time into the total run time. A ratio of 1.0, or 100 percent, would indicate that the asset was run at its best possible state. The *effective utilization index* measures how effectively the organization has used the resources at its disposal for value creation. It is calculated by dividing the standard run time into the total available time. When linked with costs, it can also indicate what the potential for cost improvement would be if the asset were operated at its full efficiency for the entire time that it was available. Figure B.1 illustrates a generic resource effectiveness model and the formulas used to calculate the efficiency and effectiveness ratios.

Although their application and nomenclature may vary from company to company, all RER models share a common conceptual framework based on industrial engineering methods. For example, a subsidiary of Pharmacia Corporation, now part of Pfizer Inc., uses a capacity reporting model similar to the one described above called the Asset Effectiveness Model (AEM). Hills Pet Nutrition uses a Resource Effectiveness Reporting Model, which is a variation of the generic RER model discussed in this section. It classifies

Figure B.1 Generic Resource Effectiveness Reporting Model

CAPACITY UTILIZATION

ACTIVITIES	CAPACITY UTILIZATION
Idle—unavailable	
Idle—unused	
Planned downtime	
Unplanned downtime	
Ancillary time	
Runtime losses	
Standard runtime	

Runtime · Available time (Available capacity) · Maximum time (Theoretical or practical capacity)

RATIOS

Utilization index = runtime ÷ available time
Efficiency index = standard runtime ÷ runtime
Effective utilization index = standard run time ÷ available time

DEFINITIONS

Runtime = Standard runtime + ancillary time + runtime losses
Available time (Available capacity) = capacity used + planned downtime + idle (unused)
Maximum time (Theoretical or practical capacity) = available capacity + idle (unavailable)

time into five major categories—policy downtime, plant decision downtime, plant downtime, run losses, and standard run time—and analyzes performance using four ratios: resource effectiveness, asset utilization, operating efficiency, and run time efficiency.[3] This model is summarized in Figure B.2.

Another variation of the RER reporting model is the *Overall Resource Effectiveness Model (ORE)*. This model measures the level of effectiveness in which a company uses all its resources, not just equipment. ORE is broken down into three categories: (1) EE—Equipment Effectiveness, which measures the percentage of time that a piece of equipment is manufacturing sellable goods; (2) HRE—Human Resource Effectiveness, which

Figure B.2 Resource Effectiveness Model at Hills Pet Nutrition

ACTIVITIES	CAPACITY UTILIZATION
Policy downtime	
Plant decision downtime	
Plant downtime	Runtime / Production available time / Plant available time / Total available time
Runtime losses	
Standard runtime	

Performance Ratios

% Resource effectivenes (Standard runtime ÷ total available time)

% Asset utilization (Standard runtime ÷ total plant available time)

% Operating efficiency (Standard runtime ÷ total production available time)

% Runtime efficiency (Standard runtime ÷ total runtime)

Adapted from Carol J. McNair and Richard Vangermeersch, *Total Capacity Management: Optimizing at the Operational, Tactical, and Strategic Levels* (New York: St. Lucie Press, 1998), pp. 80–82. Used with permission.

shows percentage of time that an individual operator is performing value-added activities; and (3) IE—Infrastructure Effectiveness, which assesses the strength of the infrastructure. ORE recognizes that effective resource utilization requires an understanding of the complex interplay among people, machines, and support systems.[4]

RER reporting systems typically do not tie resource utilization to costs. In the next section, we will discuss the CAM-I Model, which provides a specific framework for establishing this linkage. However, the methodology used in the CAM-I model can also be applied to resource effectiveness models.

THE CAM-I REPORTING MODEL

The CAM-I Reporting Model, developed by the Consortium of Advanced Manufacturing International (CAM-I), provides a framework to analyze and report capacity and link it to costs.[5] The model is seen first and foremost as a communication tool. The reporting formats are simple, easy to understand, and highlight the different levels of capacity utilization through the use of color: yellow for idle, red for nonproductive, and green for productive.

Under this model, *rated capacity*—the sum of idle, nonproductive, and productive capacity—assumes that each asset will operate 24 hours a day at its most efficient or benchmark rate. The costs of this capacity are the total costs assigned to the process. Rated capacity is the equivalent of theoretical capacity in a more traditional model.

Rated capacity drills down into more specific capacity components depending on industry and the needs of the company as follows (see Figure B.3):

○ *Idle capacity* is the sum of marketable, nonmarketable, and idle off-limits capacity.

   • *Idle marketable.* Unused capacity for which a market exists, but is currently not being used due to competitive factors, product substitutes, or other constraints such as price, cost, or distribution.

Figure B.3 CAM-I Capacity Reporting Model

Rated Capacity	Summary Model	Industry-Specific Model	Traditional Model
Rated Capacity	Idle	Not marketable	Theoretical
		Off-limits	
		Marketable	Practical
	Non-productive	Standby	Scheduled
		Waste	
		Maintenance	
		Setups	
	Productive	Process Development	
		Product Development	
		Good Products	

Adapted from Thomas Klammer, *Capacity Measurement & Improvement* (Chicago, Illinois: Irwin Professional Publishing, 1996), 17. Used with permission.

- *Idle nonmarketable.* Unused capacity for which a market does not exist or management has chosen not to participate in the particular market. This capacity is a target for abandonment or disposition.

- *Idle off-limits.* Capacity that is unavailable because of management policies or strategies such as holidays and planned shutdowns, among others.

○ *Nonproductive capacity* is the sum of those hours that are not used for productive purposes. It might include the following components:

- *Standby* capacity is the result of process variability due to customers, suppliers, or internal operations. Standby capacity results from having more capacity than the bottleneck operation or from waiting time because another operation has not provided the necessary input to the process.

- *Waste* includes scrap, rework, yield, and any other type of loss that is incurred in the process.

- *Setup* represents the cost of getting the process ready for production or service. The goal should be to minimize setup so that this time is available for productive use.

- *Maintenance* represents the work done to maintain equipment in good operating condition. Line managers usually like to distinguish between preventive and corrective maintenance. *Preventive maintenance* is planned downtime. If properly scheduled, it will create minimum disruptions to the operations. *Corrective maintenance,* by contrast, occurs unexpectedly and usually has a significant effect on the operation such as stopping the production process or requiring more employees to meet customer commitments.

○ *Productive capacity* represents resources that are used for value creation. It results in the manufacture of products or the delivery of a service according to customer expectations. It may also include the use of resources for process or product development, since these activities also create value for the customer.

The CAM-I model provides detailed information on capacity utilization that can be reported in detailed or summary form. The specific definitions within each major category (idle, nonproductive, productive) are industry specific and should be determined by management. The CAM-I model has many similarities to the Resource Effectiveness Model, reflecting their common roots in industrial engineering. The CAM-I, however, links this information to cost providing management with a tool to focus process improvements and identify areas of opportunity that will translate to the bottom line. In the next section, we will use an example of a hypothetical company called Tropical Blends to illustrate how to link capacity utilization to costs and use this information for management decision making.

HOW TO LINK CAPACITY UTILIZATION MODELS TO COSTS

Capacity reporting models can become a powerful decision support tool when linked to costs. They can present management with a clear picture of the cost of waste and underutilized resources and highlight possible areas of opportunity. Should the company increase its asset utilization by aiming for more sales, or should they focus on reducing non-value-added and support activities? The information provided by a capacity reporting model can shed insight into this issue.

The CAM-I model has proposed a framework for linking costs to capacity utilization that separates costs into those that are largely fixed (e.g., equipment and space) and those that are semivariable or variable (e.g., labor and supplies). It then assigns these costs based on the percentage of time consumed in the different activities in relation to the total hours available in the operation or facility. The following simple example will illustrate how the CAM-I framework can be used to determine capacity costs.

Tropical Blends Corporation is a manufacturing company that produces carbonated fruit drinks for local consumption and export. The bottling operation currently runs one eight-hour shift with eight employees, 5 days a week, 250 days per year. The 250-day figure considers government-mandated and company holidays. If market demand were to increase significantly, the line could operate 24 hours per day, 360 days per year. The utilization of this bottling operation during the last fiscal year is shown in Figure B.4.

Figure B.4 Capacity Utilization: Tropical Blends Corporation

CAPACITY BREAKDOWN	HOURS
Available time based on manned shifts[1]	2,000
Standard runtime	900
Runtime losses	50
Equipment setup	150
Clean-up	300
Equipment breakdown	200
Rework	100
Preventive maintenance	80
Total hours used	**1,780**
Idle—unused[2]	220
Idle—unavailable[3]	6,640
Maximum time available	**8,640**

1 Available time equals 250 workdays x 8 hour per day = 2,000
2 Idle unused = available time less total hours used = 2,000 – 1,780
3 Idle unavailable = maximum time less available time
    = (360 days x 24 hours) – 2,000 = 8,640 – 2000 = 6,640

The bottling operation incurs annual costs of $985,000, of which $685,000 represent facility and equipment costs and $300,000, labor costs. Labor costs are considered fixed costs because 8 operators are always required to run the line. Figure B.5 shows capacity reporting for Tropical Blends Corporation using the CAM-I reporting model. Facility and equipment capacity costs were based on theoretical hours and labor on available hours, since labor costs are only incurred when a shift is manned.

The cost breakdown of the CAM-I model provides detailed information on the relationship between capacity utilization and the cost structure of the organization. For example, in the category of facility and equipment costs, true cost improvement opportunities lies in the reduction of idle capacity. Idle capacity represents 80% of the total maximum time and more than $500,000 in costs. These costs eat away at the company's gross

Figure B.5 CAM-I Reporting Model for Tropical Blends Corporation

CAPACITY UTILIZATION		EQUIPMENT			LABOR		
		Hours	% Utilization	Costs*	Hours	%Utilization	Costs
Idle	Off-limits	6,640	77%	$ 527,450	–	0%	$ –
	Marketable	220	3%	20,550	220	11%	33,000
	Subtotal idle	**6,860**	**80%**	**548,000**	**220**	**11%**	**33,000**
Nonproductive	Equipment setup	150	2%	13,700	150	8%	24,000
	Clean-up	300	3%	20,550	300	15%	45,000
	Downtime	200	2%	13,700	200	10%	30,000
	Rework	100	1%	6,850	100	5%	15,000
	Preventive maintenance	80	1%	6,850	80	4%	12,000
	Run time losses	50	1%	6,850	50	3%	9,000
	Subtotal nonproductive	**880**	**10%**	**68,500**	**880**	**44%**	**132,000**
Productive	Run time (good products)	900	10%	68,500	900	45%	135,000
	TOTAL	**8,640**	**100%**	**$ 685,000**	**2,000**	**100%**	**$ 300,000**

* Equals cost per activity x % total time
For example, idle off limits = $685,000 x 32% = $527,450

margin. On the other hand, nonproductive hours in this cost category are only 10 percent of the total hours available for this operation. The cost reduction opportunity of approximately $68,500 per year pales in comparison to the opportunity to reduce costs by increasing asset utilization.

Labor also represents a cost improvement opportunity because the time spent in non-productive activities could be converted to productive uses. The reduction of non-productive time translates into cost savings because it would probably result in lower labor-related costs such as overtime and temporary labor, and may even allow for the reduction of the workweek to less than five days in the bottling operation. It would also allow the company to increase production without incurring incremental labor costs because the reduction of non-productive time liberates labor capacity and makes it available for productive uses. Nonproductive labor costs the company $132,000 per year. Improvement efforts should focus on reducing those activities that represent the largest portion of nonproductive hours—in this example, cleanup and downtime. Process inefficiencies or run time losses are only 3 per cent and therefore would not be an area of immediate focus.

The CAM-I framework can also be applied to the resource effectiveness model. Figure B.6 shows the same information reported using a generic resource effectiveness reporting model. The conclusions that can be drawn from this information are similar to the ones using CAM-I. RER presents the information in a more aggregate format and includes ratios that can be used to benchmark performance or set stretch targets. In Figure B.6, the ratios tell a simple story. The utilization index indicates that only 52.5 percent of available time is used for productive purposes. The remaining work hours are consumed by process inefficiencies, support activities, downtime, and unused capacity, which cost the company $217,850 per year. The efficiency index at 85.7 percent indicates that the process is losing $36,200 a year by running at less than its ideal state. The effective utilization index shows that if the process were operating at full efficiency during the hours that it was available, the company could save up to $254,050 per year. Based on this information, management may decide to focus on reducing downtime and support activities because the potential for cost improvement is much higher in these areas than in reducing runtime losses.

Figure B.6 Resource Effectiveness Model for Tropical Blends Corporation

CAPACITY UTILIZATION	EQUIPMENT			LABOR			TOTAL COST
	Hours	% Total Time	Cost	Hours	% Total Time	Cost	
Idle—off limits	6,640	77.0%	$527,450	–	–	$ –	$ 527,450
Idle—unused	220	3.0%	20,550	220	11.0%	33,000	53,550
Planned downtime	80	1.0%	6,850	80	4.0%	12,000	18,850
Unplanned downtime	200	2.0%	13,700	200	10.0%	30,000	43,700
Ancillary time	450	5.0%	34,250	450	22.5%	67,500	101,750
Runtime losses	150	2.0%	13,700	150	7.5%	22,500	36,200
Standard runtime	900	10.0%	68,500	900	45.0%	135,000	203,500
Maximum time	**8,640**	**100.0%**	**$685,000**	**2,000**	**100.0%**	**$300,000**	**$985,000**

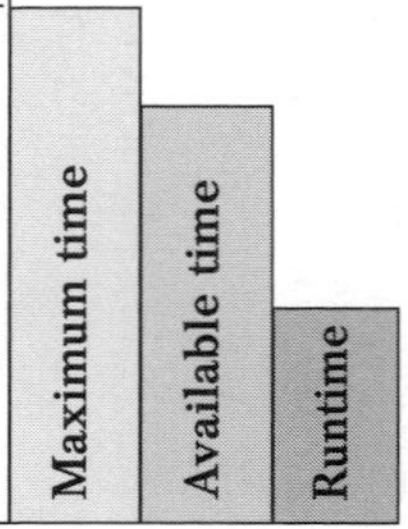

(Right side stacked labels: Maximum time / Available time / Runtime)

	Cost Opportunity	Percent	Formula
Utilization index[1]	$217,850	52.5%	(runtime ÷ available time)
Efficiency index	$36,200	85.7%	(standard runtime ÷ total runtime)
Effective utilization index[2]	$254,050	45.0%	(standard runtime ÷ available time)

Note: Runtime = Standard runtime + runtime losses = 900 + 150 = 1,050 hours
Available time = runtime + ancillary time + downtime (planned and unplanned) + idle (unused)
= 1,050 + 450 + 200 + 80 + 220 = 2,000

1 Cost opportunity utilization index = $53,550 + $18,850 + $43,700 + $101,750 = $217,850
2 Cost opportunity effective utilization index = $53,550 + $18,850 + $43,700 + $101,750 + 36,200 = $254,050

* Equals cost per activity x % total time. For example, idle off limits = $685,000 × 77% total time = $527,450.

The choice of which capacity reporting model to use will depend on the management needs and how they would like to view this type of information. Either model will present valuable information to manage the business. The information can be prepared on at different levels—by machine, work center, department, or facility—with each level providing a different view of capacity utilization for management decision making. Moreover, the use of colors to highlight idle, nonproductive, and productive capacity increase its value as a communication tool.

The REM and CAM-I model are decision-support tools that should be integrated into the performance management system of the organization. In the real world, where an operation may run multiple products and consist of several machines, the calculation of capacity costs can get quite complex. Time becomes the common denominator that can be used to assign these costs to the different capacity states.

The ultimate goal of time-based capacity reporting models is to impel the organization to act by highlighting areas of opportunity. By linking operational effectiveness and efficiency to cost information, management can determine where it should invest resources to enhance the value-added processes of the organization and lower costs.

ENDNOTES

1. Kanawaty (1992), 344–346.

2. *Changeovers* are a term used in the pharmaceutical industry, which involve a series of activities performed at the beginning and end of a production run. There are *partial changeovers*, which are performed every time a lot is manufactured, and *complete changeovers*, which are done after a fixed number of runs of the same product or when there is a product change.

3. For more information see Carol J. McNair and Richard Vangermeersch, *Total Capacity Management: Optimizing at the Operational, Tactical, and Strategic Levels* (New York: St. Lucie Press, 1998), 80–82; "Measuring the Costs of Capacity," *Statements on Management Accounting, Statement No. 4Y* (Montvale, NJ: Institute of Management Accountants, 1998), 17–19.

4. For more information on ORE, see Oded Tal, "Overall Resource Effectiveness: the Key for Cycle Time Reduction & Capacity Improvements," (GaAs Mantech, Inc., 2001), available at *www.gaasmantech.org/digest/2001*.

5. For more information on the CAM-I capacity model, see Thomas Klammer, ed., *Capacity Measurement and Improvement: A Manager's Guide to Evaluating and Optimizing Capacity Productivity* (Burr Ridge, IL: Irwin Professional Publishing, 1996) or visit the CAM-I site at *www.cam-i.org*.

Appendix C

The Use of Monte Carlo Simulations to Set Standards[1]

Traditional standards-setting methodology is afflicted with a fundamental fallacy that Dr. Sam Savage from Stanford University calls the *Flaw of Averages*. The premise is quite simple: "Plans made under the assumption that average conditions will occur are usually wrong."[2] Standards are single-point estimates that usually represent an average of the observations made of a process over a particular period of time. In Chapter 6, we discussed two types of standards that are used for costing purposes: time standards, which establish the time it should take to perform a given activity, and yield standards, which measure the efficiency in which a key input is converted into a tangible output.

Time standards are usually established by engineers or area specialists who break down a process into observable activities and measure how long it takes to complete each activity under a specific set of conditions. These individuals take a sufficient number of observations to be reasonably certain that the times are representative of the activity under evaluation. Once they gather enough data, they average the measured times for each activity over the number of observations, apply some allowances and correction factors (performance rating), and then add up all activities within a process to determine the time standard. Yields are set in a similar manner. Individuals responsible for setting yields measure the output produced of particular product or service, given a fixed level of a key input. Examples of key inputs are shown in Chapter 6 (see Figure 6.6). This output is measured over a period of time and averaged over the number of observations to determine the expected yield for the item in question.

In a perfect world, the time and yield standards should accurately reflect how inputs are converted into outputs. Unfortunately, in the real

181

world, unforeseen events and natural variation create variability, which can affect process output, capacity utilization levels, resource allocation, customer service levels, and ultimately, the financial performance of the organization. Setting standards at the average implies that a significant portion of the time you will not achieve your expected performance levels. This situation may affect your ability to meet customer commitments and deteriorate your competitive position in the market over time.

Industrial engineers typically adjust time standards to consider certain allowances for employee fatigue, equipment reliability, and other unscheduled breaks. Some companies even include a "fudge factor" in their time standards to capture the uncertainty of the critical variables affecting their process. These allowances, however, do not capture the dynamic nature of the process environment or provide information to management on how process variability affects costs and their ability to meet customer demand. So how can we incorporate the realities of an uncertain world into our standards-setting process and cost estimates?

Spreadsheet programs such as Excel are typically used to record and analyze standards data and to develop costs. However, spreadsheets are static models that show a single outcome. Accountants overcome this limitation by running alternative scenarios varying one or more key assumptions in order to assess the risk and opportunities of the situation under evaluation.

An alternative to the static spreadsheet model is the use of simulations. Simulations can provide a powerful analytical tool for examining real-life situations by systematically varying key inputs and assessing their impact on the outputs of the modeled system. The goal is to make better-informed decisions by understanding the impact of uncertainty on the key assumptions that underlie the business model.

Spreadsheet simulations use both a spreadsheet model and a simulation to analyze risk. One type of spreadsheet simulation is Monte Carlo simulation. This simulation technique generates random values for uncertain variables. Each uncertain variable has a range of possible values and a probability distribution for those values. The type of distribution selected for each variable (normal, lognormal, triangular, among others) is based on the conditions and characteristics appropriate for the process or input represented by that particular variable. These probability distributions are sampled at random within the prescribed range of values. The randomly generated values are used to create a set of scenarios that reproduce unforeseen events and the natural variability in proportion to the likelihood of their occurrence. The outcome of the simulation is a frequency distribution of output values, which shows the probability of obtaining the desired results given the uncertainty of the assumptions underlying the model.

The frequency distribution can be used to set the standard at some value other than the average. Because time standards are used to determine production plans and service schedules, the use of time standards based on averages could result in unfilled orders, late shipments, and missed schedules. Therefore, if a process has significant variability, management may wish to consider setting the standard at a higher value than the average—for example, 70 to 80 percent—to ensure its ability to meet customer requirements on a consistent basis. This decision has cost implications because the organization will have more resources than it requires on average to meet its production or service demands. For an organization operating in a standard cost environment, it would result in favorable cost variances because the actual processing time would be lower than the standard a significant portion of the time. From an operational standpoint, however, this *variability cushion* could be used to realize other important activities such as training, preventive maintenance, and documentation that are often postponed due to the day-to-day priorities of meeting production or service requirements.

From a policy standpoint, management should define whether it is more important to maintain a low cost structure and periodically miss customer requirements or meet customer expectations regularly and incur higher costs. For companies that have a high labor content or operate in an extremely competitive environment, this policy decision may place an excessive cost burden on their products or services, which cannot be compensated through increased pricing or additional sales. In other companies that have high materials content and low labor costs, the cost impact of overestimating time standards is more than offset by the incremental revenue generated from meeting customer expectations on a consistent basis.

The following example illustrates how Monte Carlo simulations can be incorporated into a real-world, standards-setting process. Island Containers is a small manufacturer of plastic products, which are sold primarily to wholesale distributors. The company recently introduced Product A, which has a market demand of 5,000 units per week and is manufactured in production runs of 1,000 units. The manufacturing process involves three major activities as shown in Figure C.1: startup, machine run time, and lot completion. Startup activities relate to the equipment setup and documentation tasks that occur at the start of each production run; lot completion activities include all tasks associated with finishing a production run. During both the startup and the lot completion activities, the machine is not operational. The machine run time is set at 80 seconds—that is, every 80 seconds, it will turn out a good unit. Two direct labor employees are required to operate the machine and maintain production flow. Once the machine starts production, the direct labor operators perform a series of parallel activities that support the production process such as unloading the machine, cleaning the units, and preparing the units for storage. The machine runs continuously 120 hours per week, and all lots must be completed by the end of the week.

The production parameters for Product A are based on results of a time study performed during the pilot runs of the product. Figure C.1 shows the average times observed for each major activity of the process. Based on these figures, the process time of Product A is 25.77 hours per lot, and the maximum amount that can be produced in any given week is five lots. Figure C.2 shows the expected cost and gross margin of Product A based on these operating assumptions. The unit cost is estimated at $2.56, which at an average selling price of $3.25 generates a healthy gross margin of 27 percent. Since market demand is 5,000 units per week, Island Containers should have no problem meeting customer requirements on a consistent basis.

The industrial engineer in charge of standards setting is concerned about the high variability observed in certain key activities, which can affect the company's ability to meet customer requirements. Although the number of sample observations is not enough to provide statistically significant data, the data provide information on process variability that can be used in a simulation model. She decides to run a Monte Carlo simulation using a program called Crystal Ball to gain a better understanding of the impact of this process variability on customer service levels and costs.[3]

The industrial engineer determines that there are three major variables affecting the output of the process: cycle time, loading materials into

Figure C.1 Production Run Parameters Product A

PRODUCTION REQUIREMENTS

Standard lot size (in units)	1,000
Direct labor employees	2

PROCESS TIME	Average	Standard Deviation	Minimum Value	Maximum Value
Cycle time (in seconds)	80	20	60	110
Start Lot				
Load materials into hopper	1.00	0.050	0.900	1.100
Enter machine parameters	0.15	0.005	0.140	0.160
Prepare documentation	0.15	0.015	0.120	0.180
Setup machine	0.50	0.025	0.350	0.600
Subtotal start lot	**1.80**	**0.095**	**1.510**	**2.040**
End Lot				
Reset machine parameters	0.08	0.008	0.070	0.090
Count units	0.75	0.150	0.500	1.000
Verify count	0.50	0.050	0.450	0.550
Document output produced	0.25	0.025	0.230	0.270
Clean area	0.17	0.025	0.140	0.200
Subtotal end lot	**1.75**	**0.258**	**1.390**	**2.110**
Total Setup Time*	**3.55**	**0.353**	**2.900**	**4.150**
Machine Time				
Run production	22.22			
Total Processing Time	**25.77**			
Net available time in hours	120			
Number of Lots per Week	**5.00**			

* Total setup time = $\sum$ Start Lot Activities + $\sum$ End Lot Activities

Figure C.2 Unit Cost Calculations for Product A

	Unit of Measure	Quantity per Lot	Cost per Unit of Measure	Total Costs
Materials	Each	500.00	$ 1.00	$ 500
Setup labor	Hours	7.10	$ 15.00	107
Labor	Hours	44.44	$ 15.00	667
Subtotal labor				774
Setup machine	Hours	3.55	$ 50.00	178
Overhead	Hours	22.22	$ 50.00	1,111
Total overhead costs				1,289
Total costs per lot[1]				**$ 2,563**
Cost per unit[2]				**$ 2.56**
Sales price				$ 3.25
Gross margin				27%

1 Sum of labor, materials, and overhead costs
2 Total costs divided by standard lot size

the hopper, and counting the units at the end of the production run. For each variable, she defines a probability distribution that will determine the range of values that will be used to run the Monte Carlo simulation. Figure C.3 shows the probability distributions for each of the uncertain variables or key assumptions. A triangular distribution was assumed for the cycle time assumption, using the minimum and maximum observed times as the upper and lower limit of the machine velocity and the average as the most likely value. For the activities of loading the materials and counting the units, a uniform distribution was used, again using the minimum and maximum observed times to set the range of possible values.[4] Four output variables are defined: the total process time, the number of lots that can be produced in a week, the unit cost, and the gross margin per unit.

Figures C.4 through C.7 show the results of a 1,000-trial simulation run. Figure C.8 shows a summary of the results and the 95 percent confi-

Figure C.3 Probability Distributions for Key Assumptions

Crystal Ball Report
Simulation started on 12/22/03 at 7:11:41
Simulation stopped on 12/22/03 at 7:11:44

Assumptions

Assumption: Cycle time (in seconds)   **Cell: B6**

Triangular distribution with parameters:

Minimum	60.00
Likeliest	80.00
Maximum	110.00

Selected range is from 60.00 to 110.00

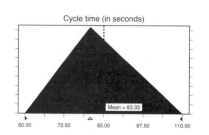

Assumption: Load materials into hopper   **Cell: B9**

Uniform distribution with parameters:

Minimum	0.90
Maximum	1.10

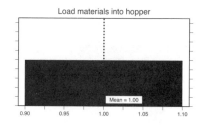

Assumption: Count units   **Cell: B17**

Uniform distribution with parameters:

Minimum	0.50
Maximum	1.00

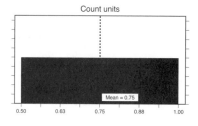

End of Assumptions

dence interval for each forecast variable. A 95 percent confidence interval provides a range of values for which there is a 95 percent probability that the forecast variable will fall within this range. Note the wide range of the possible outcomes given the variability observed in the production process. Of particular concern is the number of lots produced. Though Figure C.8 shows that the weekly output will range from 4 to 6 lots, a closer examination of the frequency distribution in Figure C.5 reveals that there is 40 percent probability of producing less than five lots a week. Based on these operating assumptions, the company would fail to meet customer requirements 40 percent of the time! In addition, the average unit cost in the simulation model is $2.63 versus $2.56 in the static model, with an average gross margin of 25 percent versus 27 percent. The use of a static model understates costs and overstates margins, potentially leading to overoptimistic projections of the financial results of the organization. How can management use this information to set the standards for this product and identify cost improvement opportunities?

Crystal Ball provides an additional tool called the *sensitivity chart* to evaluate the effect of a particular input variable on the results of the

Figure C.4 Probability Distribution for Forecast Variable:
Total Processing Time

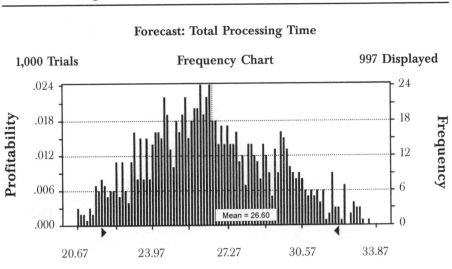

Forecast: Total Processing Time

1,000 Trials   Frequency Chart   997 Displayed

Certainty is 95.00% from 21.72 to 32.21 Hours

Figure C.5 Frequency Count for Forecast Variable: Number of Lots Processed per Week

Percentile	Number of Lots per Week
0%	4.00
10%	4.00
20%	4.00
30%	4.00
40%	4.00
50%	5.00
60%	5.00
70%	5.00
80%	5.00
90%	5.00
100%	6.00

Figure C.6 Probability Distribution for Forecast Variable: Cost per Unit

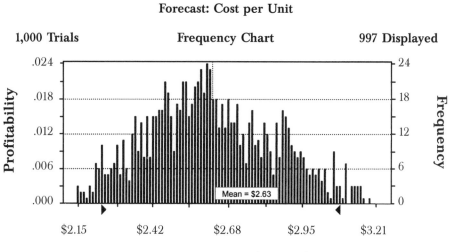

Forecast: Cost per Unit

1,000 Trials   Frequency Chart   997 Displayed

Mean = $2.63

Certainty is 95.00% from $2.24 to $3.08

Figure C.7 Probability Distribution for Forecast Variable: Gross Margin per Unit

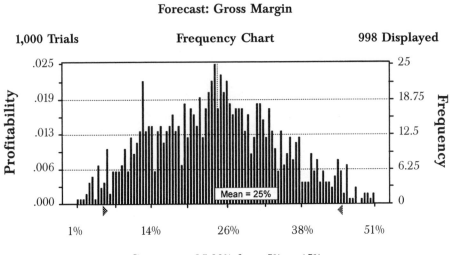

Certainty is 95.00% from 5% to 45%

Figure C.8 Summary of Monte Carlo Simulation

Forecast Variable	Low	High	Average
Process time	21.72	32.21	26.60
Number of lots	4.00	6.00	5.00
Cost per unit	$2.24	$3.08	$2.63
Gross margin per unit	5%	45%	25%

Figure C.9 Sensitivity Analysis for Number of Lots and Cost per Unit

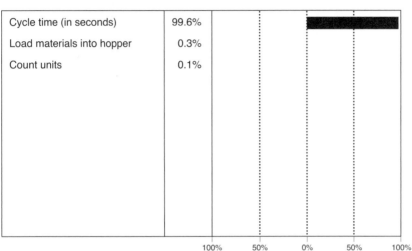

Sensitivity Chart
Target Forecast: Cost per Unit

Cycle time (in seconds)	99.6%
Load materials into hopper	0.3%
Count units	0.1%

100%   50%   0%   50%   100%

model. In our example, the largest contributor to the variance observed in the number of lots produced and unit cost is cycle time (see Figure C.9). Setup time has a negligible effect on the output of the process and the costs. Therefore, in setting the standard for the product, management could use the information generated by the Monte Carlo simulation to determine where to peg the standard. Regardless of where they decide to set the standard, significant cost variances will be generated unless they can reduce the variability in cycle time, which affects both cost and customer service. For example, if the process variability could be reduced to a range of 70 to 90 seconds per unit with an average time of 80 seconds, the company would be able to meet customer demands 100 percent of the time at an average cost of $2.56 per unit with a 95 percent probability of the unit cost falling between $2.39 and $2.74. This scenario presents a significant reduction in the volatility of unit costs from our prior range of $2.24 to $3.08 with an average cost of $2.62 per unit.

Island Containers is a very simple model to illustrate how Monte Carlo simulation can be used to understand the effects of uncertainty on capacity utilization, costs, and customer service levels. Real-world activities, products, and services will be more complex to model. The accuracy of the model used to simulate your business processes will determine the reliability of the information for decision-making purposes. In this example, I did not get into the complexities of cost behavior and how these may or may not be affected by the variability of the process. However, cost behavior would be an important factor to consider in any cost model.

Advances in computer technology have made Monte Carlo simulations accessible to any business professional with a computer and a basic understanding of statistics. Monte Carlo simulations can provide a valuable tool to move away from deterministic cost models and incorporate the effects of an uncertain environment into the operational parameters and the key inputs that drive the cost calculation. However, a user must exercise care in building the simulation model to ensure that it is representative of the business process under evaluation in a reasonably accurate manner. A poorly designed Monte Carlo simulation can actually lead a manager down the wrong path by creating a false sense of security in terms of the statistical precision of the results.

ENDNOTES

1. The author would like to thank Santos Sanabria of Pharmacia Corporation for his significant contribution to the ideas discussed in this appendix. Mr. Sanabria introduced the author to the use of Monte Carlo simulations for standard-setting purposes and showed her how to apply this context in a real-world setting to improve management decision making from a financial and operational perspective.

2. See articles by Dr. Sam Savage, "The Flaw of Averages," *San Jose Mercury News* (October 8, 2000), and "Beat the Odds: Understand Uncertainty," *Optimize Magazine* (December 2001).

3. Crystal Ball is powerful spreadsheet simulation program that functions as an Excel add-in. It is simple and easy to use. An Excel file named "AppendixC" that contains the model discussed in this appendix is available at *www.wiley.com/go/costsystems* (see "About the Web Site" in the front section of this book). The Crystal Ball program must be installed on your computer in

order to run the Monte Carlo simulation. A trial version can be downloaded free of charge at *www.decisioneering.com*. Do not try to replicate the exact results of the Monte Carlo simulation in this file. A Monte Carlo simulation generates a different set of random variables each time it is run. Therefore, the results of a particular run will be consistent, but different from a prior run.

4. A triangular distribution is a popular continuous distribution for when you have limited data but know the minimum, maximum, and most likely values. The uniform distribution is used when you know the range of possible values and all values have an equal likelihood of occurrence.

Glossary

Abnormal scrap Defective materials or units of output that are not inherent to the process and should not occur under efficient operating conditions, such as defects caused by a power outage or a lack of employee training.

Absorption variance Compares the cost of goods manufactured at standard to the actual costs incurred. It is a financial measure used by many organizations to monitor the performance of their manufacturing facilities.

Activity analysis See *work sampling*. This term is also used in activity-based costing to denote the process of analyzing the major activities of the organization and categorizing them in a meaningful manner.

Activity-based costing (ABC) A cost management approach that focuses on the activities performed in an organization. It assumes that activities consume resources and traces costs to products or services through the activities that they require.

Actual costs Costs based on actual usage and input prices.

Actual hours used The actual machine or labor hours consumed in the manufacturing or service delivery process.

Actual yield The actual output obtained from the process. It is often expressed as a percentage of the theoretical yield.

Analytical estimating A work measurement technique that combines the use of estimates and standard data. It breaks down jobs into its basic elements and then estimates or measures each one.

Ancillary time The time involved in performing key support activities that are an integral part of the process such as setup, cleanup, and changeovers.

Available capacity The maximum output that can be produced given a fixed level of resources. It is typically based on the number of manned shifts.

Available time The time the facility or equipment could work based on manned shifts. It is the equivalent of available capacity.

Balanced scorecard An integrated performance management system that translates strategies into tangible objectives and measures. It seeks to capture the value drivers of an organization by using an integrated set of performance measures to describe, communicate, and measure the strategy used for value creation.

Bill of materials File that contains a list of all components, ingredients, or raw materials to produce a finished product and the quantities required of each item.

CAM-I Reporting Model A framework developed by the Consortium of Advanced Manufacturing International (CAM-I) to analyze and report capacity and link it to costs.

Capacity The value-creating ability of the resources available to the organization or the ability of the business to meet market demand. At a micro level, it can have several definitions: (a) the value-creating potential of a process, (b) the amount of output that can be obtained from a process, (c) an upper limit or constraint on the work that an operating unit can handle, or (d) an estimate of the work done by a fixed set of resources.

Capacity utilization The extent to which a firm uses its productive capacity.

Changeovers A term used in the pharmaceutical industry to denote a series of activities performed at the beginning and end of a production run. See *partial changeovers* and *complete changeovers*.

Committed capacity costs Costs that are unavoidable in the short to intermediate term and that include items such as building rent, depreciation, security, insurance, and non-refundable service contracts.

Comparative estimating A work measurement technique that involves the identification and measurement of benchmark jobs.

Complete changeovers A term used in the pharmaceutical industry to denote a series of setup activities performed after a fixed number of runs of the same product or when there is a change from one product to another.

Confidence interval A range of values within which the true population parameter will lie. It specifies the likelihood that this interval contains the true value of the population parameter.

Confidence level The likelihood that the results from a data sample will be representative of the values of the underlying process.

Contribution margin Accounting measure that represents the difference between sales and variable costs. It represents the amount of money left over after recovering variable costs to cover fixed manufacturing costs and operating expenses. It can be calculated in total or on a per-unit basis.

Conversion costs The sum of labor and overhead costs.

Corrective maintenance Equipment repairs that are unplanned and generally disrupt the workflow.

Cost allocation base See *cost assignment base.*

Cost assignment base A factor that links the indirect costs to the item being measured.

Cost centers Organizational units whose managers are only accountable for costs; a cost center manager typically controls the inputs to the process (e.g., manpower and materials), but has no control over sales or the generation of revenue.

Cost measurement A cost system function that entails developing costs, per unit or in total, for a variety of different items and purposes.

Cost object The item to be measured or costed.

Cost pools Groups of costs that are typically used to distribute indirect costs to products or services. A cost pool can be very broad and include many cost categories such as supervisory labor, maintenance, and utilities, among others.

Cost rollup An accounting process that adds up the significant cost components and calculates the total or unit cost as required.

Costed bill of materials A bill of materials that shows the quantity required of each component, its unit cost, and the extended total cost of each component based on the usage required.

Decision support A cost system function that provides actionable cost information for decision-making purposes.

Design capacity See *practical capacity.*

Design for manufacturing and assembly (**DFMA**) A technique that focuses on making the product easier to manufacture while holding functionality levels at a predetermined level.

Direct costing See *variable costing.*

Direct costs Costs that can be identified or traced directly to a product or service.

Direct labor costs The total compensation costs of employees who work directly on manufacturing a product or providing a service to the customer. Total compensation includes wages, salaries, payroll taxes, fringe benefits, and overtime.

Downtime The time during which a process cannot be run, either for production or ancillary work, due to an interruption in the work schedule. See *planned* and *unplanned downtime.*

Effective utilization index A ratio that measures how effectively the organization has used the resources at its disposal for value creation. It is calculated by dividing the standard run time into the total available time.

Efficiency index A ratio that shows how close the asset operated to its optimal level. It is calculated by dividing the standard run time into the total run time.

Engineering Change Order (ECO) A document that constitutes a formal request for authorization to change the product or process design.

Estimating A work measurement technique that relies on the judgment and experience of the person who is making the estimates.

Expected costs Costs based on materials quantity standards, time standards, and the most current costs available for materials.

Financial reporting Cost system function that involves the preparation and reporting of financial information for management, legal, or tax purposes.

Flaw of Averages A fallacy identified with the use of averages that states that plans made under the assumption of average conditions will usually be wrong.

Forecasted costs Estimated future costs based on the best available information.

Full cost absorption A costing methodology that includes all fixed and variable costs of manufacturing as product costs. These costs are carried in inventory until sold.

Full costs An accounting term for total costs. Theoretically, it includes all costs in the value chain. In practice, it is generally the sum of the labor, materials, and overhead costs required to manufacture a product or deliver a service. In manufacturing, these costs are also known as *fully absorbed costs* or *fully burdened costs*.

Fully absorbed costs See *full costs.*

Fully burdened costs See *full costs.*

General ledger The database that contains a record of all the financial transactions of the company.

Gross margin Accounting measure that represents the difference between sales and cost of sales. It represents the amount of money left over after deducting the cost of goods sold that is available to cover operating expenses. It is usually reported on a total and per unit basis.

Idle capacity The sum of marketable, nonmarketable, and idle off-limits capacity. See *idle marketable capacity, idle nonmarketable capacity*, and *idle off-limits capacity.*

Idle marketable capacity Unused capacity for which a market exists, but is currently not being used due to competitive factors, product substitutes, or other constraints such as price, cost, or distribution.

Idle nonmarketable capacity Unused capacity for which a market does not exist or management has chosen not to participate.

Idle off-limits capacity Capacity that is unavailable because of management policies or strategies such as holidays, planned shutdowns, among others.

Idle time All hours in which employees, equipment, or facilities are available for work, but for whatever reasons are being not used.

Indirect costs Costs that are common to one or more cost objects.

Indirect labor costs The total compensation costs of those employees that support the manufacturing or service process.

Individual product cost measurement Cost system procedures that address the development of unit costs for goods manufactured.

Intangible Assets Monitor (IAM) A performance management model based on the concept of the knowledge organization. It provides a mechanism for measuring intangible assets and presenting relevant indicators in a simple manner.

Inventory valuation Accounting procedure that involves the periodic allocation of production cost between cost of goods sold and inventory.

Investment (I) A term used in theory of constraints to denote the money invested in inventory or those items that the system intends to sell.

Item master File that contains detailed information about all components, subassemblies, and finished products used or manufactured by the organization.

Labor hours available per employee The productive time available per employee after subtracting planned allowances for a particular time period.

Labor standards The estimated time an employee should take to complete an operation.

Last costs The most current costs available for the resources consumed in the manufacturing or service-delivery process.

Maintenance The work done to keep the equipment in good operating condition.

Managed capacity costs Costs that are avoidable in the short to intermediate term and typically include labor, utilities, and supplies, among others.

Material usage factor See *scrap factor.*

Maximum capacity See *theoretical capacity.*

Maximum time The maximum possible time the process is available for production or service within a given period. It is equivalent to *theoretical* or *practical* capacity, depending on how it is defined by the organization.

Mean A measure of central tendency that represents an average of the sample observations, the historical data points, or the results of several pilot runs.

Median A measure of central tendency that represents the middle value in a series of observations arranged in ranked order.

Method study A technique that records and examines the work involved in performing a particular task in order to make improvements.

Mixed scenario The use of two separate overhead rates for calculating product or service costs: one for committed costs based on practical capacity and another for managed costs based on available capacity.

Mode A measure of central tendency which represents the observation that occurs most frequently and is not affected by order or differences of scale.

Monte Carlo simulation A technique that uses random number generation to reproduce alternate scenarios based on certain assumptions as defined by the user. It allows users to incorporate variability and risk into their decision models and provides a tool to better understand the probability of specific outcomes and to identify the key variables that are driving the results.

Nonproductive capacity The sum of those hours that are not used for productive purposes.

Normal operating conditions The typical environment in which a product is manufactured or the service delivery process takes place. It should consider the common allowances and delays that occur during the process.

Normal scrap Materials losses that are inherent to the production process and arise even under efficient operating conditions. They are included in the product cost.

Ockham's razor A principle that states a theory should be as simple as possible to explain a phenomenon.

Operating expense (OE) A term used in theory of constraints that is defined as the money spent to convert investment into throughput.

Operational control Cost system procedures or reports that provide feedback to managers on the resources consumed.

Outliers Data points or observations that are radically different from the rest and are not considered representative of the process.

Overall Resource Effectiveness Model (ORE) A variation of the Resource Effectiveness Reporting Model (RER) that measures the level of effectiveness in which a company uses all its resources, not just equipment.

Overhead costs Indirect costs that cannot be directly traced to a product or service in a cost-effective manner.

Overhead pools See *cost pools.*

Part parent A finished product or the top level in the product hierarchy.

Partial changeovers A term used in the pharmaceutical industry to denote a series of setup activities performed every time a lot is manufactured.

Performance management A cost system function that links operational measures, resource utilization, and costs to help manage organizational performance.

PFD allowance An allowance that considers personal time such as bathroom breaks, fatigue, and delay in setting time standards. PFD is usually expressed as a percentage of the standard time and is added to the time allowed for the specific task being measured.

Planned allowances The expected number of hours that an employee or a process is not available for work due to company policies or procedures.

Planned capacity See *scheduled capacity.*

Planned downtime An interruption to the process that can be planned in advance, such as preventive maintenance, employee training, or communication meetings.

Practical capacity The level of output that can be obtained from a particular operation given the current process specifications and the system design.

Preventive maintenance Maintenance that, if properly scheduled, will create minimum disruptions to the operations.

Process manufacturers Manufacturing organizations that produce like products in a continuous manner.

Process time The time required to complete a particular operation.

Product hierarchy The order of manufacture or assembly as shown in the bill of materials.

Product structure See *bill of materials.*

Productive capacity The resources that are used for value creation.

Profit centers Organizational units evaluated based on the operating or net income of the particular subunits of the organization. Ideally, a profit center manager should influence all major factors affecting revenues and costs, such as pricing, sales and marketing strategies, and sources of supply.

Project facilitator An individual that provides direction and focus to the project team.

Project leader An individual that is part of the project team and acts as the main point of contact with the rest of the project team on a day-to-day basis. This person may also be the project facilitator.

Projected costs See *forecasted costs.*

Quality function deployment (QFD) A technique that ensures that the customer requirements are not compromised during the design process.

Range The difference between the maximum value and the minimum value in the data set.

Rated capacity The sum of idle, nonproductive, and productive capacity.

Rating A method used to adjust an individual's performance up or down based on the normal pace that has been defined for a particular task or operation.

Resource Effectiveness Reporting Models (RER) Capacity reporting models based on industrial engineering concepts that focus primarily on machine utilization.

Rework Units of production that do not meet customer specifications and are subsequently repaired.

Routing File that contains the sequence of operations that will be performed on the product and the detailed labor hours, machine hours, and setup time that will be required by each operation.

Run time The time the process is actually running. It is the available time less any downtime, idle time, or ancillary time.

Run time losses The loss of available hours as a result of process inefficiencies, such as running an automated line at a slower pace than the standard rate.

Scheduled capacity The amount of output that is projected for a particular time period.

Scrap Unusable materials or production units (whether partially or fully completed) that do not meet customer requirements. These materials or units must be either sold at a minimal value or disposed of in a safe and reasonable manner.

Scrap factor A factor used to adjust the bill of materials (and the related materials cost) for components that are damaged or spoiled in the process.

Semivariable costs Costs that have a fixed and variable component. Maintenance, electricity, and water are examples of semivariable costs.

Sensitivity chart A chart used to evaluate the effect of a particular input variable on the results of a Monte Carlo simulation.

Setup time The preparation time involved in the production or service delivery process. It may involve equipment installation, documentation, entering run parameters, clean-up, and other miscellaneous activities at the start and the end of a process.

Skandia Navigator A proprietary performance measurement model used by Skandia Corporation to manage their intellectual capital.

Standard costs Expected costs that serve as goals to be achieved and are expressed on a per unit basis. They are based on materials quantity standards, time standards, and the expected costs of labor, materials, and other inputs for a particular time period.

Standard deviation A statistic that shows how the data are scattered around the mean. It is a measure of dispersion or variability.

Standard run time The amount of time that the organization takes to produce the product or service under efficient operation conditions.

Standard yield The expected good output based on a level of input and process efficiency.

Standby capacity Available unused capacity that results from process variability due to customers, suppliers, or internal operations.

Steering committee A group of individuals that oversees the planning and implementation of a major project.

Step-fixed costs Costs that increase in discrete steps beyond a certain level of output. These costs remain fixed within an established range and increase in a step-like fashion when output exceeds this range.

Structured estimating A work measurement technique that uses the experience of the estimator, but imposes a structure and discipline on the estimating process so that it produces more reliable results.

Subassembly A intermediate product that is used in the manufacture of the end product.

Theoretical capacity Represents the maximum amount of work that a process or facility can produce operating 24 hours per day, 7 days per week, with zero waste.

Theoretical yield The maximum good output for a particular process based on a fixed level of input and the established process design.

Theory of constraints (TOC) A methodology developed by Eli Goldratt that involves identifying the system constraint, deciding how to optimize its use, and subordinating all other elements of the system to the constraining factor.

Throughput (T) Sales less totally variable costs.

Throughput accounting (TA) A cost management approach based on the theory of constraints that focuses on three major measures: throughput, inventory, and operating expenses.

Time study A traditional work measurement technique used by industrial engineers to set time standards. It involves dividing the process being studied into its basic elements and measuring the time it takes to complete each task.

Totally variable costs Costs that increase or decrease in direct proportion to the output sold.

Turnkey applications Information systems applications designed and developed by third-party vendors, which can be customized through the system setup to different types of businesses.

Unavailable capacity Hours that are not manned due to policy constraints or market conditions.

Unavoidable delays A provision for unscheduled interruptions such as equipment reliability and any other factors that might affect the production or service delivery process.

Unavoidable operator allowance A provision for operator fatigue and any other unscheduled breaks that may affect labor productivity.

Unplanned downtime Interruption to the process that cannot be planned in advance and that disrupts the workflow such as equipment breakdowns, power outages, and materials shortages.

Utilization index A ratio that measures the proportion of total hours the asset was utilized for productive purposes in relation to the total available time.

Value engineering (VE) A technique that seeks to maximize customer value by increasing functionality and quality while simultaneously reducing costs.

Variable costing An accounting method that expenses fixed overhead costs to the income statement in the period incurred. It contrasts with full cost accounting in which fixed overhead costs are carried in inventory until the item is sold.

Variance The difference between the actual costs incurred and standard, budgeted, or forecasted costs.

Variance analysis The process that examines the differences between the actual costs incurred and the standard, budgeted, or forecasted costs to identify opportunities for cost improvement.

Waste Any type of loss that is incurred in the process such as scrap, rework, and yield.

Work measurement A technique that determines the time required for a qualified worker to perform a task working at a given pace.

Work sampling A work measurement technique that involves making sufficient observations of an employee's activities to determine the relative amount of time this person spends on the various activities associated with the process or task at hand.

Yield A measure of process efficiency. It represents the output that can be produced given a fixed level of input.

Yield factor A factor used in the bill of materials to account for the expected loss under efficient or normal operating conditions. It is expressed as a percent of the material input into the process. The yield factor not only affects materials cost, but also any conversion costs that have been applied to up to that stage of the process.

References

2003 Survey of Management Accounting. Ernst & Young, 2003.

Aft, Lawrence S. *Work Measurement & Methods Improvement.* New York: John Wiley & Sons, Inc., 2000.

Berlant, Debbie, Reese Browning, and George Foster. "How Hewlett-Packard Gets Numbers It Can Trust." *Harvard Business Review* (January–February 1990): 178–183.

Berliner, Callie, and James A. Brimson, eds. *Cost Management for Today's Advanced Manufacturing: The CAM-I Conceptual Design.* Boston: Harvard Business School Press, 1988.

Breen, Ken, Gary Pecora, Dave Gregerson, and Tom McCabe. "A New Direction: Integrated Management Systems." *Quality Digest* (August 1997).

Brimson, James. *Activity Accounting: An Activity-Based Costing Approach.* New York: John Wiley & Sons, Inc., 1991.

Brinker, Barry J., ed. *Emerging Practices in Cost Management.* Boston: Warren, Gorham & Lamont, 1990.

Buttross, Thomas E., Hal Buddenbohm, and Dan Swenson. "Understanding Capacity Utilization At Rocketdyne." *Management Accounting* (Winter 2000).

Chase, Richard B. and Nicholas J. Aquilano. *Production and Operations Management: A Life Cycle Approach.* Homewood, IL: Richard D. Irwin, Inc., 1989.

Cochran, Craig. "Using Quality Objectives to Drive Strategic Performance." *Quality Digest* (November 2000).

Cokins, Gary, Alan Stratton and Jack Helbling. *An ABC Manager's Primer.* Montvale, NJ: Institute of Management Accountants, 1992.

Corbett, Thomas. *Throughput Accounting.* Great Barrington, MA: The North River Press, 1998.

Cooper, Robin. "You Need a New Cost System When...." *Harvard Business Review* (January–February 1989): 77–82.

———. "The Two-Stage Procedure in Cost Accounting: Part One." *Journal of Cost Management* (Summer 1987): 43–51.

———. "The Two-Stage Procedure in Cost Accounting: Part Two." *Journal of Cost Management* (Fall 1987): 39–45.

Cooper, Robin, and Robert S. Kaplan. "Measure Costs Right: Make the Right Decisions." *Harvard Business Review* (September–October 1988): 96–103.

Cooper, Robin, Robert S. Kaplan, Lawrence S. Maisel, Eileen Morrissey, and Ronald M. Oehm. *Implementing Activity-Based Cost Management: Moving from Analysis to Action.* Montvale, NJ: Institute of Management Accountants, 1992.

Crosby, Phil B. *Quality Is Free: The Art of Making Quality Certain.* New York: Penguin Books, 1979.

———. *Quality Without Tears: The Art of Hassle-Free Management.* New York: McGraw-Hill, 1984.

Deming, W. Edwards. *Out of the Crisis.* Boston: MIT Press, 2000.

"Developing Comprehensive Performance Indicators." *Statements on Management Accounting, Statement No. 4U.* Montvale, NJ: Institute of Management Accountants, 1995.

The Economist Numbers Guide: The Essentials of Business Numeracy. New York: John Wiley & Sons, Inc., 1997.

Evans, James R. *Essentials of Business Statistics.* Upper Saddle River, NJ: Pearson Education, Inc., 2003.

Goldratt, Eliyahu M., and Jeff Cox. *The Goal.* Great Barrington, MA: North River Press, 1992.

Gray, Anne E., and James Leonard. "Capacity Analysis: Sample Problems." *Harvard Business School Note #9-606-058.* Boston: Harvard Business School Publishing, 1995.

Hammer, Michael, and James Champy. *Reengineering the Corporation.* New York: HarperCollins Publishers, 1993.

Hayes, Robert H., and Steven C. Wheelwright. *Restoring our Competitive Edge, Competing Through Manufacturing*. New York: John Wiley & Sons, Inc., 1984.

Heskett, J.L., Thomas O. Jones, Gary W. Loveman, W. Earl Sasser, Jr., and Leonard A. Schlesinger. "Putting the Service-Profit Chain to Work." *Harvard Business Review*. (March–April 1994): 164–174.

Hope, Jeremy, and Fraser, Robin. *Beyond Budgeting: How Managers Can Break Free from the Annual Performance Trap*. Boston: Harvard Business School Press, 2003.

Horngren, Charles T., and George Foster. *Cost Accounting: A Managerial Emphasis*. Englewood Cliffs, NJ: Prentice-Hall, Inc., 1991.

Horngren, Charles T., George Foster, and Srikant M. Datar. *Cost Accounting: A Managerial Emphasis*. Englewood Cliffs, NJ: Prentice-Hall, Inc., 1997.

Horngren, Charles T., George Foster, and Srikant M. Datar. *Cost Accounting: A Managerial Emphasis*. Englewood Cliffs, NJ: Prentice-Hall, Inc., 2003.

"Implementing Activity-Based Management: Avoiding the Pitfalls." *Statements on Management Accounting, Statement No. 4CC*. Montvale, NJ: Institute of Management Accountants, 1998.

"Implementing Capacity Cost Management System." *Statements on Management Accounting, Statement Number 4LL*. Montvale, NJ: Institute of Management Accountants, 2000.

Ishikawa, Kaoru. *What Is Total Quality Control?* Englewood Cliffs, NJ: Prentice-Hall, 1985.

Johnson, H. Thomas, and Robert S. Kaplan. *Relevance Lost: The Rise and Fall of Management Accounting*. Boston: Harvard Business School Press, 1987.

———. *Relevance Regained: From Top-Down Control to Bottom-Up Empowerment*. New York: The Free Press, 1992.

Kanawaty, George. *An Introduction to Work Study*. 4th ed. Geneva, Switzerland: International Labour Office, 1992.

Kaplan, Robert S. "The Four-Stage Model of Cost Systems Design." *Management Accounting* (February 1990): 22–27.

———. "One Cost System Isn't Enough." *Harvard Business Review* (January–February 1988): 61–66.

Kaplan, Robert S., ed. *Measures for Manufacturing Excellence.* Boston: Harvard Business School Press, 1990.

Kaplan, Robert S., and Robin Cooper. *Cost & Effect: Using Integrated Costs Systems to Drive Profitability and Performance.* Boston: Harvard Business School Press, 1998.

———. "The Promise and Peril of Integrated Cost Systems." *Harvard Business Review* (July–August 1998): 109–119.

Kaplan, Robert S., and David P. Norton. *Balanced Scorecard: Translating Strategy into Action.* Boston: Harvard Business School Press, 1996.

———. "The Balanced Scorecard—Measures that Drive Performance." *Harvard Business Review* (January–February 1992): 71–79.

———. "Putting the Balanced Scorecard to Work." *Harvard Business Review* (September–October 1993): 134–142.

———. *The Strategy-Focused Organization: How Balanced Scorecard Companies Thrive in the New Business Environment.* Boston: Harvard Business School Press, 2000.

Klammer, Thomas, ed. Capacity *Measurement and Improvement: A Manager's Guide to Evaluating and Optimizing Capacity Productivity.* Burr Ridge, IL: Irwin Professional Publishing, 1996.

Kohnler, Eric L. *A Dictionary for Accountants.* Englewood Cliffs, NJ: Prentice-Hall, Inc., 1975.

McNair, Carol J., and Richard Vangermeersch. *Total Capacity Management: Optimizing at the Operational, Tactical, and Strategic Levels.* New York: St. Lucie Press, 1998.

"Measuring the Costs of Capacity." *Statements on Management Accounting, Statement No. 4Y.* Montvale, NJ: Institute of Management Accountants, 1998.

Niven, Paul R. *Balanced Scorecard Step-By-Step: Maximizing Performance and Matching Results.* Hoboken, NJ: John Wiley & Sons, Inc., 2002.

Noreen, Eric, Debra Smith, and James T. Mackey. *The Theory of Constraints and Its Implications for Management Accounting.* Great Barrington, MA: North River Press, 1995.

Oliver, Lianabel. *The Cost Management Toolbox: A Manager's Guide to Controlling Costs and Boosting Profits.* New York: AMACOM, 2000.

Pande, Peter S., Robert P. Nueman, Roland R. Cavanagh. *The Six Sigma Way, How GE, Motorola, and Other Top Companies Are Honing Their Performance.* New York: McGraw-Hill, 2000.

Porter, Michael E. *Competitive Advantage: Creating and Sustaining Superior Performance.* New York: The Free Press, 1985.

"Practices and Techniques: Implementing Activity-Based Management: Avoiding the Pitfalls." *Statements on Management Accounting, Statement No. 4CC.* Montvale, NJ: Institute of Management Accountants, 1998.

"Roles and Practices in Management Accounting Today." *Strategic Finance* (July 2003).

Savage, Sam. "The Flaw of Averages." *San Jose Mercury News* (October 8, 2000).

———. "Beat the Odds: Understand Uncertainty." *Optimize Magazine* (December 2001).

Schemann, William A. and John Lingle. "Seven Greatest Myths of Measurement." *Management Review* (May 1997): 29–32.

Schmenner, Roger W. *Service Operations Management.* Englewood Cliffs, NJ: Prentice-Hall, Inc., 1995.

Simmons, Sylvia. *How to Be the Life of the Podium: Openers, Closers & Everything in Between to Keep Them Listening.* New York: AMACOM, 1991.

Standard Costs and Variance Analysis. Montvale, NJ: Institute of Management Accountants, 1974.

Stevenson, William J. *Production/Operations Management.* Homewood, IL: Richard D. Irwin, Inc., 1990.

"Theory of Constraints." *Statements on Management Accounting, Statement No. 4HH.* Montvale, NJ: Institute of Management Accountants, 1999.

"Tools and Techniques for Implementing Integrated Performance Systems." *Statements on Management Accounting, Statement No. 4DD.* Montvale, NJ: Institute of Management Accountants, 1998.

Turney, Peter B. *Common Cents.* Hillsboro, OR: Cost Technology, Inc., 1991.

Walton, Mary. *The Deming Management Method.* New York: The Putnam Publishing Company, 1986.

———. *Deming Management at Work.* New York: The Putnam Publishing Company, 1990.

Weisman, Dennis L. "How Cost Allocation Systems Can Lead Managers Astray." *Journal of Cost Management* (Spring 1991): 4–10.

West, John E. (Jack). "Three Strategies for Aligning Quality Policies, Objectives and Processes." *Quality Digest* (June 2002).

Upton Jr., Wayne S. "Business and Financial Reporting, Challenges from the New Economy." *Financial Accounting Series Special Report No. 219A.* Norwalk, CT: Financial Accounting Standards Board, April 2001.

Yu-Lee, Reginald Tomas. *Essentials of Capacity Management.* Hoboken, NJ: John Wiley & Sons, Inc., 2002.

Index